I0012583

The Python Blueprint:

A Hands-on Approach to

Conquer Python Programming

from Scratch

First of all, let me say congratulations and welcome to the exciting journey you're about to embark on. By picking up this book, you've taken the first step towards learning a valuable skill that has the potential to open up incredible opportunities. This isn't just a book about Python programming—it's about unlocking a new way of thinking, solving problems, and creating amazing things.

Now, you may be wondering, "Why Python?" There's a simple answer: it's powerful, it's versatile, and it's in demand. Python is a language used by hobbyists and tech giants alike—it powers everything from simple task automation to artificial intelligence and machine learning. It's even used in scientific research and space exploration!

But don't let that intimidate you. One of the reasons Python is loved worldwide is its simplicity. It's beginner-friendly with syntax that reads almost like English. So, even if you're new to programming or if the word "algorithm" sounds like a strange, exotic animal, don't worry. You're in good hands.

In this book, we'll start by getting you familiar with the fundamental concepts of programming—algorithms, data structures, and all the good stuff. We'll then dive into the basics of Python, introducing you to variables, data types, loops, and conditions. Don't sweat it if these terms seem unfamiliar now; they will become your best friends as we proceed.

Next, we'll introduce you to the world of functions and modules, which will take your Python skills to a new level. Then, we'll venture into the more advanced topics like object-oriented programming and handling files and exceptions in Python.

Once we've laid the groundwork, the real fun begins! We'll delve into data manipulation, analysis, and visualisation with Python's powerful libraries. We'll also venture into the world of web scraping and automation. If you've ever dreamed of commanding your computer to automatically do tasks for you, you're in for a treat.

Following this, we'll put your newfound knowledge into practice with some intermediate projects. This will give you a feel for what real-world Python programming is like. We'll then open the doors to Python's application in web development and machine learning. We'll even build a simple website and machine learning model together.

Throughout this journey, we'll make sure we emphasise the best practices in Python, so not only will you be able to code, you'll be able to code well.

Don't worry if all this sounds a bit overwhelming right now. We're going to take it step-by-step, and I promise you, it's going to be an exciting ride. The world of Python programming is a world of constant discovery and problem-solving, full of challenges but also full of rewards.

Remember, learning to code is like learning a new language or a musical instrument. It's not about getting it perfect the first time—it's about practice, patience, and persistence. So don't be afraid to make mistakes or get stuck. It's all part of the process.

So, are you ready to become a Pythonista? Are you ready to embark on this journey of discovery? If so, turn the page and let's dive in. Welcome to your new adventure.

Programming Concepts

As we embark on our coding adventure, it's important that we get to grips with some fundamental concepts. Consider this like setting up base camp before a mountain climb. We'll dig into what programming is, understand how computers work, decipher programming languages, explore algorithms and data structures, and underline the importance of code efficiency. Ready? Let's get started!

What is Programming?

Think of programming as a form of communication, a way to tell a computer what to do. At its core, programming is about problem-solving—you have a problem and you need to instruct the computer on how to solve it. However, computers don't understand human languages. They only comprehend the language of binaries, ones and zeros. This is where programming languages come in—they allow us to write instructions in a way that both we and computers can understand. Programming, at its heart, is all about making computers solve problems efficiently.

How Computers Work

Now, you might be wondering how computers execute these instructions. Inside every computer is a processor, its "brain". This processor carries out the instructions in your code, one after the other. It can do calculations, remember information, and control other parts of the computer.

But how does it "remember" things? This is where memory comes in. The computer's memory, or RAM, stores information that the processor may need to refer to. It's like the processor's scratch pad—it notes down important stuff while it works. This intricate dance between the processor and memory is what allows a computer to perform complex tasks, like showing you this page!

Understanding Programming Languages

As mentioned earlier, programming languages bridge the gap between human and computer languages. They fall into two main categories: low-level languages, which are closer to the binary code computers understand directly, and high-level languages, which are closer to human languages. Python, for example, is a high-level language—it abstracts away many complexities and lets us write code that's relatively easy to read.

What is an Algorithm?

When we talk about problem-solving, we're usually referring to algorithms. An algorithm is a step-by-step procedure to solve a problem or achieve a specific outcome. It's like a recipe—if you follow the steps correctly, you'll end up with a tasty dish (or in our case, a solved problem). Just like there are countless recipes for cookies, there can be numerous algorithms to solve a problem, but some can be more efficient than others.

Understanding Data Structures

Data structures are the containers in which we store data. They help us organise, process, and manage data efficiently. Think of them as different types of boxes; some boxes are better for storing a certain type of item, some are easier to search within, some are easier to rearrange. In programming, we have various data structures like lists, arrays, queues, stacks, trees, and more. Each has its strengths and weaknesses and is best suited to a particular type of problem.

Speaking of efficiency, this brings us to a critical concept in programming— time and space complexity. Time complexity is a measure of the amount of time an algorithm takes to run. Space complexity is a measure of the amount of memory an algorithm needs to run. As programmers, we strive for efficiency—we want our code to run as quickly as possible, using as little memory as possible. Efficient code is particularly important when dealing with large amounts of data or when resources are limited.

Understanding these fundamentals will set you up nicely for the journey ahead. It's a lot to take in, but remember, it's not a race. Take your time to digest these concepts. Don't worry if you don't get everything immediately—like all good things

Software Development

Software development is a fascinating field that encompasses a wide array of activities involved in creating and maintaining software applications. It merges the power of computing with creative problem-solving, making it a captivating endeavour for individuals with a knack for technology and innovation.

Software development can take on various forms, each catering to a different facet of the digital world we inhabit. For instance, web development focuses on building websites and web applications that are typically hosted on the internet or an intranet. It's split into two main categories: front-end (or client-side) development which deals with the elements of a website users interact with, and back-end (or server-side) development which handles the server, application, and database that work behind the scenes to power the website.

Mobile development, on the other hand, revolves around creating software applications for mobile devices. This could include anything from the apps we use daily on our smartphones, like social media or fitness tracking apps, to enterprise-level applications used by businesses.

Game development is a specialised field of software development dedicated to creating video games for computers, gaming consoles, and mobile devices. It often involves a combination of coding, graphic design, and sound design.

Moreover, data science and machine learning development use software development skills to analyse data and build predictive models, often used in decision-making processes in various industries.

A typical software project follows a specific workflow, generally encapsulated by the software development life cycle (SDLC), which includes stages such as planning, analysis, design, development, testing, deployment, and maintenance. This process ensures the software is built systematically, meeting the desired requirements while mitigating potential errors.

Within a software development team, you'll find various roles, each contributing a unique set of skills. The software developer or programmer writes the code that makes up the software. The software architect makes high-level design choices and sets the technical standards. The project manager oversees the project, ensuring it stays on schedule and meets its objectives. The quality assurance analyst tests the software for defects, while the UX/UI designers ensure the software is user-friendly and intuitive.

Understanding these elements of software development provides a strong foundation for embarking on a rewarding journey in this field. As we delve into Python programming, we'll see how these principles come into play, aiding us in not only writing code but creating software solutions that solve real-world problems.

Introduction

Before we dive into the nitty-gritty, let's address the elephant in the room: Why Python? After all, there are many programming languages out there. What makes Python special? Why should it be your first (or next) language of choice? In the following sections, we'll discuss Python's characteristics as a high-level language, its versatility, and the ever-growing Python community.

Why Learn Python?

High-Level Language

Before we proceed, it's important to understand what we mean when we refer to Python as a high-level language. The programming world often distinguishes between two categories: high-level and low-level languages, with each having distinct features and uses.

Low-Level Languages: These are languages that are closer to the machine language, which is the fundamental language that computers understand (binary code composed of ones and zeros). Low-level languages like assembly language or C, offer a deep level of control over the system hardware. They allow the programmer to manage the memory and processor usage precisely, which can lead to more efficient code. However, they also demand a detailed understanding of the computer architecture and come with a steep learning curve. Additionally, low-level languages require significant amounts of code to perform even the simplest tasks.

High-Level Languages: On the other hand, high-level languages like Python, Java, and JavaScript, stand at the opposite end of this spectrum. They abstract away many of the complexities associated with machine language, providing a more human-friendly interface. High-level languages are designed to be easily read and written by humans, not machines, making them more intuitive and accessible for beginners. They handle many of the intricate, tedious details of the computer, such as memory management, enabling developers to focus more on problem-solving and logic, which are the crux of programming.

Python epitomises the qualities of a high-level language. Its syntax is not only clean but also incredibly readable. In fact, Python's syntax is frequently compared to English due to its straightforward style, which is punctuated with clear, expressive commands. This readability makes Python an excellent choice for beginners as it allows them to grasp the fundamentals of programming without getting bogged down in complex syntax.

Unlike some languages that can be quite verbose, Python strives for simplicity and minimalism. It encourages writing less code for achieving the same task, which boosts productivity and reduces the likelihood of errors. Python also promotes writing "beautiful" code—code that is readable, simple, and concise, leading to more maintainable and robust software.

When you learn Python, you're not just learning a programming language. You're adopting a mindset that values simplicity, readability, and efficiency, a philosophy that can benefit you in all areas of software development.

Learning Python is more than just understanding the syntax; it's about absorbing a philosophy, a way of problem-solving, that will serve you well across your programming journey. Python offers a gateway into the world of programming, and by learning it, you're setting yourself on a path to software mastery. And this is just the beginning. In the following sections, we'll explore the versatility of Python and the vibrant community surrounding it—further reasons that add to Python's allure.

Versatility

A key aspect of Python that makes it an alluring language for many is its extraordinary versatility. Think of Python as a Swiss Army knife in the realm of programming languages—it's a single tool, packed with a wide array of features, capable of tackling myriad tasks with ease.

Despite its simplicity, Python's capabilities are anything but basic. Its applications span across numerous domains, making it not just the Jack of all trades, but remarkably, the master of many. Whether you're interested in web development, game design, data analysis, machine learning, or scientific computing, Python has a place in your toolkit.

Web and Game Development

In web development, Python's easy-to-read syntax and robust web frameworks—like Django and Flask—make building everything from simple web applications to complex, feature-rich websites a streamlined process. For game development, libraries like Pygame provide a platform for Python developers to bring their creative ideas to life.

Data Analysis and Machine Learning

Python's versatility shines especially bright in the fields of data analysis and machine learning. Libraries such as pandas and NumPy offer powerful tools for data manipulation and analysis. For machine learning and AI, Python is almost the de facto language of choice. Libraries like scikit-learn, TensorFlow, and PyTorch provide the capabilities to design sophisticated machine learning algorithms and models.

Scientific Computing

In the realm of scientific computing, Python is valued for its precision and efficiency. Libraries like SciPy and Matplotlib facilitate complex mathematical calculations and data visualisations. Whether you're conducting intricate quantum physics simulations or predicting weather patterns, Python delivers reliable results.

Automation and More

Beyond these domains, Python is frequently used for automation tasks. Be it web scraping using Beautiful Soup or automating mundane tasks using Python scripts, it's all within reach. With Python, you can automate email sending, excel calculations, and even your daily computer tasks.

Extensive Libraries and Modules

A significant part of Python's versatility comes from its extensive standard library, which covers a wide array of programming tasks, from file I/O and system operations to Internet protocols and web services. Moreover, if you can't find what you need in the standard library, there's a good chance that someone has developed a third-party library or module for it. Python's vibrant community continually develops and supports an incredible wealth of packages, which can extend Python's capabilities even further.

Growing Community

Finally, a key strength of Python lies in its community. Having a strong, active community is a huge asset for a programming language. The Python community is vast, supportive, and constantly growing. This means that if you ever run into issues (which, spoiler alert, you will—it's part of the learning process), there are countless forums, blogs, and resources where you can seek help. It's like having an extended family of Pythonistas ready to lend a hand.

Furthermore, the community continuously contributes to Python's growth by developing new libraries and frameworks, making Python an excellent choice for cutting-edge fields like machine learning and data science.

So, why Python? Well, it's beginner-friendly yet powerful, versatile across various domains, and backed by a passionate, supportive community.

Python is more than just a programming language—it's a tool that can open doors to countless opportunities.

Installation and Setup

Python can be installed on various operating systems, including Windows, Linux, and MacOS. Let's look at each in turn.

Windows: To install Python on Windows, head to the official Python website (www.python.org) and download the latest version of Python for Windows. Run the downloaded .exe file and follow the instructions. Make sure to tick the box that says "Add Python to PATH" during installation. This allows you to run Python from any command prompt.

Linux: Many Linux distributions come with Python pre-installed. To check if Python is installed, open a terminal and type "python3 --version". If Python is installed, you'll see the version number. If not, you can install it using your distribution's package manager, such as apt for Ubuntu.

MacOS: Like Linux, MacOS often comes with Python pre-installed, although it might not be the latest version. To install a newer version, you can use the Homebrew package manager, or download it from the Python website as with Windows.

Remember, learning to code is like learning to cook—you need the right tools. But instead of pots and pans, we use interpreters and text editors.

How to Use Python Interpreter and Text Editors

Using IDLE

Python comes with its own environment called IDLE (Integrated Development and Learning Environment). IDLE is simple and easy to use, making it great for beginners. To launch it, just search for "IDLE" in your computer's start menu or application launcher.

Text Editors: Atom, Sublime Text, VS Code

As you get more comfortable with coding, you might want to switch to a more feature-rich text editor. Atom, Sublime Text, and VS Code are popular choices. These text editors are versatile, supporting various programming languages and offering features like auto-completion, easy navigation, and the ability to manage multiple files and projects. You can download any of these from their respective websites, then open them and start coding by creating a new file with a .py extension.

Jupyter Notebooks

What is Jupyter Notebook?

Jupyter Notebook is an open-source web application that allows the creation and sharing of documents containing live code, equations, visualisations, and explanatory text. It's part of the Project Jupyter, a non-profit project that aims to provide open tools for interactive and reproducible computing.

The Notebook has support for over 40 programming languages, including Python, R, Julia, and Scala. The name "Jupyter" is a combination of Julia, Python, and R. It provides a unique blend of both a rich text editor and an interactive programming environment.

Jupyter Notebooks are composed of cells, which can be of three types: Code, Markdown, and Raw.

Code cells: These cells contain code to be executed by the kernel. The programming language used is based on the kernel, for instance, a Python kernel will run Python code cells.

Markdown cells: These cells contain text formatted using markdown and are used to provide documentation or guide for the notebook.

Raw cells: These cells are not executed by the notebook. They are included, for example, when converting the notebook to different formats using nbconvert.

Working with Jupyter Notebook

To get started with Jupyter Notebook, you first need to install it. The easiest way is by installing the Anaconda Distribution which includes Python, Jupyter Notebook, and other commonly used packages for scientific computing and data science.

Once installed, you can start a new Jupyter notebook by opening your terminal or command prompt and typing jupyter notebook. This will open the Jupyter interface in your default web browser.

From the Jupyter interface, you can create a new notebook by clicking on 'New' and selecting the kernel (like Python 3). Once the notebook opens, you'll see a cell where you can start writing code or text.

For example, if you write print("Hello, World!") in a code cell and hit Shift + Enter, the code will execute, and you'll see the output underneath.

You can add more cells, change cell types, and much more using the toolbar or keyboard shortcuts. You can also save the notebook, and it will be saved as a .ipynb file, which you can reopen later or share with others.

One of the powerful features of Jupyter notebooks is that you can include plots from libraries like matplotlib or seaborn and the plots will be displayed in the notebook itself, making it excellent for data exploration and interactive visualisation.

Google Colab

Google Colab, or "Colaboratory", is a free cloud-based service provided by Google, much like Jupyter Notebook. It allows users to write and execute Python code through the browser without any configuration or the need for powerful hardware. It's especially favored among data scientists and Machine Learning practitioners for its pre-installed libraries and free GPU access.

What is Google Colab?

Google Colab is a Jupyter notebook environment that runs entirely in the cloud. It doesn't require any setup, and you can access it through your Google Drive. You can use it to write and execute code, build reproducible documentation, and share your work.

One major advantage of Google Colab is that it provides free access to GPU (Graphics Processing Unit) and TPU (Tensor Processing Unit) for computations, making it a very attractive option for running machine learning and deep learning models.

Google Colab supports most of the commonly used Python libraries, and they come pre-installed. It also provides easy access to files in your Google Drive and easy integration with GitHub.

Working with Google Colab

You can start a new Colab notebook directly from your Google Drive by clicking on 'New' > 'More' > 'Google Colaboratory', or you can visit the Colab website and create a new notebook.

A Colab notebook, like a Jupyter notebook, consists of cells which can be either code cells or text cells. You can write Python code in a code cell and then run the code using Shift + Enter. The output will be displayed immediately below the cell.

You can switch the runtime type to include a GPU by clicking on 'Runtime' > 'Change runtime type' and selecting 'GPU' from the dropdown menu.

For example, if you write print("Hello, World!") in a code cell and hit Shift + Enter, the code will execute, and you'll see the output underneath.

You can import files from your Google Drive or from your local file system. To import a file from Google Drive, you can use the Google Colab's drive module:

```
from google.colab import drive
drive.mount('/content/drive')
```

After running this code, you'll be provided with a link to get an authorisation code. Once you have the code, enter it into the box, and your Google Drive will be mounted for use in the notebook.

Colab notebooks can be shared just as you would with Google Docs or Sheets. Simply click the 'Share' button at the top right of the screen, and you can give others access to view or edit your notebook.

Basic Syntax and Comments

With your Python environment set up, it's time to delve into Python's syntax and the role of comments in your code. Both are fundamental aspects of Python programming.

Python Syntax

Indentation: Unlike many other languages, Python uses whitespace (spaces and tabs) to delimit blocks of code. Where other languages like Java or C++ use braces {} to define a block of code, Python uses indentation. Typically, a code block following an if statement, for instance, or defining a function, is indented four spaces or one tab.

Variables: Variables are declared simply by assigning a value to them. Unlike languages like C or Java where you have to explicitly declare the type of a variable, Python infers the type based on the value assigned to it. For example, you can declare a variable x and assign it the integer value 4 by writing x = 4. Python's flexibility in variable declaration simplifies the coding process by eliminating the need for explicit type declarations.

Loops and Control Flow: Python uses intuitive English keywords for its control flow constructs, such as for, while, if, else, and elif. This design choice enhances the readability of the code, making it more accessible to beginners. For instance, the keyword "for" is used to iterate over a sequence of elements, "while" is used for looping based on a condition, and "if", "else", and "elif" are used for conditional execution of code blocks.

Functions: Functions are defined using the keyword "def", followed by the function name and parentheses (). The parentheses may contain parameters that the function accepts, allowing you to pass values into the function for processing. Functions enable code reuse and modularisation, allowing you to define reusable blocks of code that can be called and executed at various points within your program.

Objects and Classes: Python is an object-oriented programming language, meaning it supports the concepts of objects and classes. Objects are instances of classes, which are user-defined structures that encapsulate data and behaviours. In Python, classes are defined using the keyword "class". They serve as blueprints for creating objects with specific attributes and methods. By utilising objects and classes, you can organise your code into logical units, promoting code reusability, maintainability, and abstraction.

Commenting Your Code

Comments are an essential part of your code. They are used to describe what the code does and how it works, and they are especially crucial when working on projects with others. Even when you're working alone, comments can help you remember your thought process when you return to a piece of code after some time.

In Python, comments are written after a # symbol. Everything after the # on that line is considered a comment and is ignored by the Python interpreter. For example:

```
# This is a comment in Python

x = 4  # This is an inline comment
```

Multi-line comments are typically written as multiple single-line comments:

```
# This is a multi-line comment.

# It is written as multiple single-line comments.
```

Alternatively, you can use triple quotes (either """ or ''') to start and end multi-line comments, though this is less common:

```
"""

This is another way to write

a multi-line comment in Python

"""
```

Understanding Python's basic syntax and the role of comments are fundamental first steps in learning to code in Python. While the syntax gives you the rules you need to write code, comments give you the ability to annotate your code to enhance its understandability. Both will be integral components of your Python programming journey.

Basics of Python

Data Types

Python, like other programming languages, supports a variety of data types. Understanding these is crucial as they form the building blocks of your code.

Numbers

In Python, we primarily work with three numerical types: integers, floating-point numbers, and complex numbers.

Integers: used to represent whole numbers without any fractional component. They can be positive, negative, or zero. Examples of integers include 3, -1, and 5000. In Python, you can create an integer simply by writing the number without any decimal point. For instance, you can assign the value 3 to a variable by writing x = 3. Integers in Python have no size limitation, allowing you to work with numbers of any magnitude within the memory constraints of your system.

Floats: short for "floating-point numbers," are used to represent numbers with a decimal point or a fractional component. They are capable of representing real numbers, including both whole numbers and numbers with decimal values. Examples of floats include 3.14, -0.01, and 1.0 (which is equivalent to the integer 1). In Python, you can create a float by explicitly including a decimal point in the number. For example, you can assign the value 3.14 to a variable by writing x = 3.14. Floats allow for more precise representation of values but come with a trade-off in terms of computational efficiency and potential rounding errors due to the limited precision of floating-point arithmetic.

Complex numbers: Complex numbers are numbers that have both a real component and an imaginary component. The imaginary component is represented using the imaginary unit, denoted as "j" in Python. Complex numbers can be expressed in the form a + bj, where "a" represents the real part and "b" represents the imaginary part. For example, 3 + 2j is a complex number with a real component of 3 and an imaginary component of 2. In Python, you can create complex numbers by directly specifying the real and imaginary parts using the syntax a + bj. Complex numbers in Python can be used to perform advanced mathematical operations and are particularly useful in fields such as signal processing and scientific computing.

String: In Python, a string is a sequence of character data. It is used to represent textual information such as words, sentences, or even entire documents. Strings are enclosed in quotes, and you can use either single quotes ('Hello') or double quotes ("Hello") to define a string, as long as the opening and closing quotes match. For example, "Hello, World!" and 'Python Programming' are both valid strings in Python. Strings can contain letters, numbers, symbols, and even whitespace characters. They can also be empty, meaning they contain no characters at all. Python provides a wide range of built-in methods and operators to manipulate and work with strings effectively.

List: A list in Python is an ordered collection of items. It is a mutable data type, which means you can modify its content after it has been created. Lists are defined by enclosing a comma-separated sequence of objects within square brackets []. The items in a list can be of different types, including numbers, strings, other lists, or even more complex objects. For example, [1, 2, 3] and ['apple', 'banana', 'orange'] are both valid lists in Python. Lists allow you to store and access multiple elements using indexing, slicing, and various list methods. They are versatile and widely used in Python for tasks such as storing data, implementing data structures, and managing collections of related information.

Tuple: A tuple in Python is similar to a list, but it is immutable. This means that once a tuple is defined, you cannot change its content. Tuples are defined by enclosing a comma-separated sequence of objects within parentheses (). For example, (1, 2, 3) and ('apple', 'banana', 'orange') are both valid tuples in Python. Like lists, tuples can contain elements of different types. Tuples are useful when you want to store a collection of values that should not be modified, ensuring data integrity and immutability. Tuples are often used to represent related information that should remain constant, such as the coordinates of a point or the RGB values of a colour.

Dictionary: A dictionary in Python is an unordered collection of key-value pairs. It provides a way to store and retrieve data based on unique keys. Dictionaries are defined by enclosing a comma-separated list of key-value pairs within curly braces {}. Each key-value pair is separated by a colon (:), where the key represents the identifier or label for the associated value. For example, {'name': 'John', 'age': 25} is a dictionary where 'name' is the key and 'John' is the corresponding value. Keys in a dictionary must be unique, and they are typically strings, but they can also be numbers or other immutable types. Dictionaries allow for efficient lookup and retrieval of values based on their keys, making them ideal for tasks such as data mapping, configuration settings, and organising structured data.

Set: A set in Python is an unordered collection of unique items. It is used to store a collection of distinct elements, where each element occurs only once within the set. Sets are defined by enclosing a comma-separated list of items within curly braces {}. Unlike lists or tuples, sets do not maintain any specific order for their elements. For example, {1, 2, 3} and {'apple', 'banana', 'orange'} are both valid sets in Python. Sets are particularly useful when you want to eliminate duplicate values from a collection, perform mathematical set operations like union, intersection, and difference, or test membership of an element within a group. Sets are mutable, allowing you to add or remove items, and they can contain elements of different types, as long as they are immutable.

Type Conversion

Python provides several built-in functions for converting one data type to another. Here are some common examples:

- int(x) converts x to an integer.
- float(x) converts x to a float.
- str(x) converts x to a string.
- list(x) converts x (typically a sequence, like a string, tuple, or set) to a list.
- tuple(x) converts x to a tuple.
- set(x) converts x to a set.

```
# Converting a float to an integer

float_number = 3.14

integer_number = int(float_number)

print(integer_number)  # This will output: 3


# Converting a string to an integer

string_number = "5"

integer_number = int(string_number)

print(integer_number)  # This will output: 5
```

Understanding Python's data types and how to convert between them is essential. You'll find that many problems in Python programming involve manipulating these data types in various ways. So get comfortable with these data types—they're some of the most powerful tools in your Python toolbox!

Variables and Operators

In this section, we'll cover two fundamental concepts in Python programming: variables and operators. A strong understanding of these is critical as they form the core of many Python programs.

Variables

Variables are identifiers that are used to store values in memory. In Python, a variable is created the moment you first assign a value to it. For example:

```
x = 10  # x is a variable storing the integer value 10

message = "Hello, Python!"  # message is a variable storing a
string
```

Variables don't need to be declared with any particular type, and can change type after they've been set.

Arithmetic Operators

Arithmetic operators are used to perform mathematical operations like addition, subtraction, multiplication, etc.

- Addition (+): x + y adds x and y.
- Subtraction (-): x - y subtracts y from x.
- Multiplication (*): x * y multiplies x by y.
- Division (/): x / y divides x by y.
- Modulus (%): x % y returns the remainder of the division of x by y.
- Exponentiation ():** x ** y raises x to the power of y.

- Floor Division (//): x // y divides x by y, rounding down to the nearest whole number.

Assignment Operators

Assignment operators are used to assign values to variables. The simplest assignment operator is =, as in x = 5. But Python also supports combined assignment and arithmetic operators:

- x += 5 is equivalent to x = x + 5
- x -= 5 is equivalent to x = x - 5
- x *= 5 is equivalent to x = x * 5
- And so forth for /=, %=, **=, and //=.

Comparison Operators

Comparison operators are used to compare two values and return a Boolean value (True or False).

- Equal (==): x == y returns True if x equals y.
- Not equal (!=): x != y returns True if x is not equal to y.
- Greater than (>): x > y returns True if x is greater than y.
- Less than (<): x < y returns True if x is less than y.
- Greater than or equal to (>=): x >= y returns True if x is greater than or equal to y.
- Less than or equal to (<=): x <= y returns True if x is less than or equal to y.

Logical Operators

Logical operators are used to combine conditional statements:

- and: Returns True if both statements are true.
- or: Returns True if at least one of the statements is true.
- not: Reverse the logical state of the operand.

Bitwise Operators

Bitwise operators act on operands as if they were strings of binary digits.

- & (AND): Sets each bit to 1 if both bits are 1.
- | (OR): Sets each bit to 1 if one of two bits is 1.
- ^ (XOR): Sets each bit to 1 if only one of two bits is 1.
- ~ (NOT): Inverts all the bits.
- << (Left Shift): Shift left by pushing zeros in from the right and letting the leftmost bits fall off.
- >> (Right Shift): Shift right by pushing copies of the leftmost bit in from the left and letting the rightmost bits fall off.

Membership Operators
Python's membership operators test for membership in a sequence, such as strings, lists, or tuples.

- in: Evaluates to true if it finds a variable in the specified sequence and false otherwise.

- not in: Evaluates to true if it does not finds a variable in the specified sequence and false otherwise.

```
# List of fruits

fruits = ["apple", "banana", "cherry", "date"]


# Use the 'in' operator to check if 'apple' is in the list

if "apple" in fruits:

    print("Apple is in the list!")

else:

    print("Apple is not in the list!")


if "grape" not in fruits:

    print("Grape is not in the list!")

else:

    print("Grape is in the list!")
```

Conditional Statements

Conditional statements in Python allow you to test conditions and perform different actions depending on whether those conditions are true or false.

If Statement: The if statement is used to test a specific condition. If the condition is true, the block of code under the if statement will execute. For example:

```
x = 10
if x > 0:
    print("x is positive")
```

In this example, because x is indeed greater than 0, the message "x is positive" is printed.

Else Statement: The else statement is used in conjunction with the if statement to handle the situation when the if condition is false. For example:

```
x = -5
if x > 0:
    print("x is positive")
else:
    print("x is not positive")
```

Here, because x is not greater than 0, the message "x is not positive" is printed.

Elif Statement: The elif statement (short for "else if") is used to chain multiple conditions. For example:

```
x = 0
if x > 0:
    print("x is positive")
elif x == 0:
    print("x is zero")
else:
    print("x is negative")
```

In this example, because x equals 0, the message "x is zero" is printed.

Looping Statements

Looping statements in Python are used to repeatedly execute a block of code.

For Loop: The for loop in Python is used to iterate over a sequence (like a list, tuple, dictionary, string, or set) or other iterable objects. Iterating over a sequence is called traversal. For example:

```
for i in range(5):
    print(i)
```

This for loop prints the numbers 0 through 4, each on a new line.

While Loop: The while loop in Python is used to iterate over a block of code as long as the test expression (condition) is true. For example:

```
i = 0
while i < 5:
    print(i)
    i += 1
```

This while loop does the same thing as the for loop in the previous example: it prints the numbers 0 through 4.

Remember, it's crucial to ensure that your loops eventually reach a condition where they stop to prevent infinite loops, which can crash your program.

Control Statements

Control statements in Python allow you to manipulate the course of your code's execution based on certain conditions or breakpoints. These include the break, continue, and pass statements.

Break Statement: The break statement in Python terminates the current loop and resumes execution at the next statement, just like the traditional "break" found in C. It is useful when you've performed a condition check in a loop and want to exit the loop when the condition is met. For example:

```
for i in range(10):
    if i == 5:
        break
    print(i)
```

This code will print numbers from 0 to 4. When i equals 5, the break statement is encountered and the loop terminates.

Continue Statement: The continue statement in Python returns the control to the beginning of the current loop. When encountered, the loop's current iteration is stopped, and it proceeds with the next one. It is beneficial when you want to skip a particular iteration of the loop. For example:

```python
for i in range(10):
    if i == 5:
        continue
    print(i)
```

This code will print all numbers from 0 to 9, except for 5. When i equals 5, the continue statement is encountered, and the current iteration is skipped.

Pass Statement: Pass is a placeholder statement in Python. It doesn't change the program's flow but is syntactically needed. It's often used as a placeholder where code will eventually go but has not been written yet. For example:

```python
for i in range(10):
    if i == 5:
        pass    # A place holder for code to be written in the future.
    print(i)
```

This code will print all numbers from 0 to 9, including 5. The pass statement doesn't do anything. It's just a placeholder for where code could potentially go.

Control statements like break, continue, and pass give you greater command over how your code executes, allowing for more complex and efficient Python programs. Understanding these will help you manipulate your code's control flow more effectively.

Python Built-in Functions
Basic Functions:

- print() function is used to print the specified message or data to the screen.

```python
print("Hello, Python!")
```

- input() function allows user input. You can assign the user's input to a variable.

```python
name = input("What's your name? ")
```

- type() function returns the type of the specified object.

```python
x = 5
print(type(x))  # This will output: <class 'int'>
```

- len() function returns the number of items in an object.

```python
list = [1, 2, 3, 4]
print(len(list))  # This will output: 4
```

Math Functions:

- abs() returns the absolute value of a number.
- min() returns the smallest of all provided arguments.
- max() returns the largest of all provided arguments.
- round() rounds a number to the nearest integer, or to the specified number of decimals if that's provided.
- pow() returns the value of one number raised to the power of another.

User-Defined Functions

In addition to built-in functions, Python also allows you to create your own functions. This is where your programming can become more advanced and nuanced.

Function Definition and Calling: To define a function, use the def keyword, followed by the function name and parentheses. The code block within every function is indented. You call a function simply by typing the function name followed by parentheses.

```
def greet():  # This is how you define a function.

    print("Hello, Python!")


greet()  # This is how you call a function.
```

Return Statement: The return statement is used to exit a function and go back to the place from where it was called. It can also send a result back to the caller.

```
def square(x):

    return x ** 2


print(square(5))  # This will output: 25
```

Function Arguments: You can send information into a function by using function arguments. These are specified after the function name, inside the parentheses.

```
def greet(name):  # 'name' is a function argument

    print(f"Hello, {name}!")


greet("Python")  # This will output: Hello, Python!
```

Lambda Function: A lambda function is a small anonymous function. It can take any number of arguments, but can only have one expression.

```
multiply = lambda a, b: a * b

print(multiply(5, 6))  # This will output: 30
```

Python Modules

A module in Python is a file containing Python definitions and statements. It allows you to logically organise your Python code, making the code easier to understand and use.

What is a Module?

A module is a file containing Python definitions and statements. The file name is the module name with the suffix .py added.

Built-in Modules: Python comes with a library of standard modules. Some of these, which are universally useful, are built into the interpreter; others are written in Python and are part of the standard library.

- math: This module provides mathematical functions. For example, math.sqrt(x) returns the square root of x.

- random: This module implements pseudo-random number generators for various distributions including integer and float.

- datetime: This module supplies classes for manipulating dates and times.

Import Statement

The import statement is used to add a module to your project, so you can use its functions, classes, and variables.

Importing a Module: To import a module, just type import followed by the name of the module. Once a module is imported, you can use its functions by using the dot (.) operator. For example:

```
import math
print(math.sqrt(25))  # This will output: 5.0
```

From-Import Statement: If you only need certain functions from a module, you can use the from keyword to import only those. For example:

```
from math import sqrt

print(sqrt(25))  # This will output: 5.0
```

In this case, you don't need to use the dot operator before the function name.

Import with renaming: Sometimes, for the sake of readability, you might want to rename a module when you import it. You can do this with the as keyword. For example:

```
import datetime as dt

print(dt.date.today())
```
In this example, dt is now an alias for datetime. Any time you want to use a datetime function, you just use dt instead.

Python's modules, and the ability to import them into your projects, allow you to use powerful, pre-existing functions and classes that can significantly increase the efficiency and effectiveness of your programming.

Advanced Topics

Object-Oriented Programming (OOP)

Object-oriented programming (OOP) is a programming paradigm that is based on the concept of "objects". Objects are instances of classes, which can contain data, in the form of fields (also known as attributes), and code, in the form of procedures (also known as methods).

Understanding Classes and Objects: In Python, everything is an object, and each object is an instance of a class. Classes provide a means of bundling data and functionality together. You can define a class using the class keyword.

```
class Dog:

    def __init__(self, name, age):

        self.name = name

        self.age = age


    def bark(self):

        print("Woof woof!")
```

Here, Dog is a class with attributes name and age, and a method bark(). You can create an instance of the class, or an object, like this:

```
my_dog = Dog("Fido", 3)

my_dog.bark()  # This will output: Woof woof!
```

Inheritance

In object-oriented programming (OOP), inheritance allows us to create new classes based on existing classes. It is a mechanism that enables a class to inherit properties and behaviours (methods and attributes) from a parent class, known as the base or superclass. The newly created class is called the derived or subclass.

By using inheritance, we can define a hierarchy of classes, where the derived classes inherit the characteristics of the parent class. This promotes code reuse and allows us to create more specialised classes without duplicating code. The derived classes can add their own specific features or override the inherited methods to provide different implementations.

For example, consider a base class called "Animal" with methods like "eat" and "sleep." We can create derived classes such as "Cat" and "Dog" that inherit these methods. The derived classes can then add their own unique methods or modify the inherited methods to suit their specific behaviour, such as "meow" for the Cat class and "bark" for the Dog class.

Polymorphism

A fundamental concept in OOP, refers to the ability of an object to take on multiple forms or exhibit different behaviours depending on the context. It allows objects of different classes to be treated as objects of a common parent class. This flexibility is achieved through inheritance and method overriding.

With polymorphism, we can write code that operates on objects of a superclass, and it will work seamlessly with objects of any derived class. This concept is based on the principle of substitutability, where objects of different classes can be used interchangeably as long as they share a common interface or inheritance hierarchy.

For example, consider a superclass called "Shape" with a method called "area." We can have multiple subclasses like "Rectangle" and "Circle" that inherit from the Shape class and implement their own version of the "area" method. By treating objects of these subclasses as objects of the Shape class, we can call the "area" method on them without needing to know the specific subclass. This allows us to write generic code that can work with various shapes interchangeably.

Encapsulation

Encapsulation is a principle in OOP that involves bundling data and the methods that operate on that data into a single unit, known as a class. It provides a way to hide the internal state and implementation details of an object from external entities. The encapsulated data can only be accessed or modified through the methods defined in the class, ensuring proper control and protection.

Encapsulation helps in achieving data abstraction, data hiding, and data security. It allows us to create classes with well-defined interfaces, where the internal workings and complexities are hidden from other parts of the program. This simplifies the usage and maintenance of the codebase.

For example, consider a class called "BankAccount" with private variables like "balance" and methods like "deposit" and "withdraw." The private variables are encapsulated within the class, and external entities cannot directly access or modify them. Instead, they interact with the account through the public methods, which provide controlled access to the encapsulated data.

Abstraction

Abstraction is a fundamental concept in OOP that involves simplifying complex systems by focusing on the essential aspects while hiding unnecessary details. It allows us to create abstract representations of real-world entities or concepts in the form of classes and objects.

Abstraction is achieved by defining interfaces, abstract classes, and methods that provide a high-level view of the functionality without revealing the underlying implementation. The details that are not relevant to the current context are abstracted away, promoting modularity, flexibility, and maintainability.

For example, consider a class hierarchy representing different types of vehicles: Car, Truck, and Motorcycle. Each of these classes may have methods like "start_engine" and "accelerate," but the specific implementation details may vary. By creating an abstract class called "Vehicle" and defining these common methods as abstract methods, we can provide a high-level abstraction of the functionality shared by all vehicles. The concrete subclasses can then implement these methods according to their specific needs.

Abstraction helps in managing complexity, providing clear interfaces for interaction, and facilitating code reuse by promoting modular design and encapsulation.

In conclusion, inheritance, polymorphism, encapsulation, and abstraction are core concepts in object-oriented programming that enable code reuse, flexibility, modularity, and maintainability. Understanding and effectively utilising these concepts can lead to well-structured, extensible, and efficient software development.

Exception Handling

Exception handling is a key aspect of building robust Python applications. Errors and exceptions are unavoidable in any codebase, and it's crucial to be able to predict, manage, and handle these issues elegantly instead of letting your program crash.

To clarify, errors and exceptions are different things in Python. Errors are problems in the code that stop execution and cannot be recovered from, like a Syntax Error when you forget an indentation or a bracket. Exceptions, on the other hand, are events that occur during the execution of the program, and they can be handled.

Understanding Exceptions

At its core, an exception is an event that occurs during the execution of a program, causing a disruption in the normal flow of the program's instructions. This could be due to logical errors, incorrect data, unavailable resources, or a host of other issues. For example, trying to open a file that doesn't exist raises a FileNotFoundError, and trying to divide a number by zero raises a ZeroDivisionError. These are both examples of exceptions.

Exceptions are not inherently bad; in fact, they're incredibly useful. They signal that something exceptional has happened, and they provide a lot of context about what exactly went wrong, including a traceback to the line where the exception was raised.

In Python, exceptions are instances of classes deriving from the base class Exception. There is a hierarchy of exception classes in Python, allowing for different categories and types of exceptions that you can catch and handle.

When an exception is raised in your program, Python will stop executing the rest of the current function, and it will keep interrupting the flow of your program until it either exits the program entirely (in which case you'll see a traceback and an error message in your console), or until it encounters an appropriate exception handler.

Handling Exceptions

To prevent a program from stopping when an exception occurs, you can use try...except statements to catch and handle exceptions.

```
try:

    print(10 / 0)

except ZeroDivisionError:

    print("You can't divide by zero!")
```

Try, Except, Finally Blocks

The try block is used to enclose the code that might throw an exception. The except block is used to catch and handle the exception(s) that are encountered in the try block. The finally block is a place to put any code that must execute, whether an exception was raised or not.

Raising Exceptions

In Python programming, exceptions are raised when errors occur at runtime. We can also manually raise exceptions using the raise keyword.

```
x = -5

if x < 0:

    raise Exception("Sorry, no numbers below zero")
```

File Handling

Python provides several functions for creating, reading, updating, and deleting files. The open() function is used to open a file, and it returns a file object that has methods and attributes for getting information about and manipulating the file.

Working with Files

Here's a basic example of opening and closing a file in Python:

```
f = open("test.txt")  # Open file in current directory

f.close()  # Close the file
```

Reading from a File

To read the content of a file, use the read() method:

```
f = open("test.txt")

print(f.read())

f.close()
```

Writing to a File

To write to an existing file, you must add a parameter to the open() function, like 'a' (append) or 'w' (write):

```
f = open("test.txt", 'w')

f.write("This is a test.")

f.close()
```

File Modes

Python provides several modes for opening a file, like 'r' (read), 'a' (append), 'w' (write), and 'x' (create). By default, the open() function opens a file for reading.

Handling CSV and TXT Files

Python has a built-in CSV library for reading and writing CSV files. For TXT files, you can use the regular file handling functions.

Regular Expressions

Regular expressions, also known as regex or regexp, are a powerful tool for working with text. They are essentially a tiny language for describing patterns in strings. They're used in programming languages, including Python, for tasks like checking whether a string matches a pattern, extracting substrings of interest, replacing parts of a string, and more. In this chapter, we'll explore what regular expressions are and how they can be used in Python.

What are Regular Expressions?

Regular expressions are sequences of characters that form a search pattern. This pattern can be used to match, find, or replace text in a string. Regular expressions can be simple, such as abc which matches any string containing "abc", or complex with special characters and quantifiers, such as ^a.*z$ which matches any string that starts with "a" and ends with "z".

Here are some common regular expression symbols:

- '.': Matches any character except newline.
- '*': Matches zero or more occurrences of the preceding character.
- '+': Matches one or more occurrences of the preceding character.
- '?': Matches zero or one occurrence of the preceding character.
- '^': Matches the start of a string.
- '$': Matches the end of a string.
- '[abc]': Matches any of the characters a, b, or c.
- '[a-z]': Matches any lowercase letter.
- '\d': Matches any decimal digit.

Regular Expressions in Python

In Python, the re module provides regular expression support. Here are some common re module functions:

match(): Determines if the regular expression matches at the beginning of the string.

search(): Searches the string for a match to the regular expression, returning a match object, or None if no match was found.

findall(): Returns all non-overlapping matches of the regular expression as a list of strings.

sub(): Replaces one or many matches with a string.

Here's an example of how you might use regular expressions in Python:

```python
import re
# Search for the pattern "123" in a string
match = re.search("123", "abc123def")
print(match.group())  # Outputs: 123
# Replace any occurrence of "123" with "456"
replaced = re.sub("123", "456", "abc123def")
print(replaced)  # Outputs: abc456def
# Find all three-digit numbers in a string
numbers = re.findall("\d\d\d", "abc123def456")
print(numbers)  # Outputs: ['123', '456']
```

In these examples, we use simple patterns for illustrative purposes. However, regular expressions allow for much more complex patterns, including combinations of special characters, character classes, quantifiers, and more.

It's important to note that regular expressions can be quite complex and tricky to get right, especially for more complex patterns. Use tools like online regular expression testers to help build and test your regular expressions.

Functional Programming in Python

Functional programming is all about immutability, no side effects, and higher-order functions.

Immutability: In functional programming, once a variable is set, you can't change it. While Python doesn't enforce this strictly, you can adopt this principle in your Python programs.

No Side Effects: Functions in functional programming don't have side effects—they don't change anything in the world around them. They take inputs and produce outputs without changing the input or any data that is not local to the function.

Higher-Order Functions: These are functions that accept other functions as arguments, return a function as a result, or both. Python's map(), filter(), and reduce() functions are examples of higher-order functions.

Map, Filter, Reduce Functions

Map: The map() function applies a given function to each item of an iterable and returns a list of the results.

```
numbers = [1, 2, 3, 4, 5]

squares = map(lambda x: x ** 2, numbers)

print(list(squares))  # Outputs: [1, 4, 9, 16, 25]
```

Filter: The filter() function constructs a list from elements of an iterable for which a function returns true.

```
numbers = [1, 2, 3, 4, 5]

evens = filter(lambda x: x % 2 == 0, numbers)

print(list(evens))  # Outputs: [2, 4]
```

Reduce: The reduce() function applies a binary function (a function that takes two arguments) to the items of an iterable in a cumulative way. For example, if you wanted to calculate the product of all numbers in a list, you could use reduce(). Note that reduce() is in the functools module.

```
from functools import reduce


numbers = [1, 2, 3, 4, 5]

product = reduce(lambda x, y: x * y, numbers)

print(product)  # Outputs: 120
```

In these examples, we use lambda functions, which are small anonymous functions that are defined with the lambda keyword. They can be very handy for functional programming in Python.

Functional programming in Python may not seem idiomatic, and Python certainly isn't a pure functional language like Haskell. However, understanding these concepts can help you write more readable and testable code by encouraging a more declarative style of programming.

Python Standard Library

The Python Standard Library is a collection of modules and packages that are included with Python. These libraries provide a lot of functionality, such as file I/O, system calls, string management, Internet protocol handling, and more.

Understanding the Standard Library

The standard library is a set of modules included with every Python distribution. It's important to familiarise yourself with the standard library because it can help you solve a wide range of problems.

Commonly Used Libraries

Here are a few commonly used libraries from the Python Standard Library:

- os: This module provides a way of using operating system dependent functionality, like reading or writing to the environment, managing files and directories, and more.
- sys: This module provides access to some variables used or maintained by the Python interpreter and to functions that interact strongly with the interpreter.
- json: This module provides an easy way to encode and decode data in JSON. JSON (JavaScript Object Notation) is a popular data interchange format.
- csv: This module implements classes to read and write tabular data in CSV format.

Advanced Python Libraries

Scipy

SciPy is a free and open-source Python library that is used for scientific and technical computing. SciPy contains modules for optimisation, linear algebra, integration, interpolation, special functions, FFT, signal and image processing, ODE solvers, and other tasks common in science and engineering.

Built on the NumPy framework and its array objects, which allows for efficient storage and manipulation of numerical arrays. This makes SciPy suitable for mathematical algorithms and convenience functions built on top of NumPy structures.

The library is organised into sub-packages covering different scientific computing domains. These are clusters, constants, Fourier transforms, integration, interpolation, I/O, linear algebra, miscellaneous routines, ndimage, ODE solvers, optimisation, signal processing, sparse matrices, special functions, statistical distributions and functions, and wavelets.

Using SciPy

Before you can use SciPy, you need to install it. This can usually be done with a simple pip command: pip install scipy. Since SciPy is built on NumPy, you'll need to have NumPy installed as well.

```
# Importing SciPy

import scipy
```

Here's an example of how to use SciPy for a basic task, solving a linear algebra problem. Let's say we have the following set of linear equations:

```
3x + 2y = 18

x - y = 2
```

We can represent these equations in matrix form (Ax = B), and use the scipy.linalg.solve() function to find x:

```
# Importing the required modules

from scipy import linalg

import numpy as np

# Define the coefficient matrix `A` and `B`

A = np.array([[3, 2], [1, -1]])

B = np.array([18, 2])

# Solve the system of equations

x = linalg.solve(A, B)

print(x)
```

This will output the solutions for x and y.

SciPy is a powerful tool in the Python ecosystem for scientific and technical computing. It leverages the power of NumPy arrays and includes many useful modules for various scientific computing applications. As a beginner, you'll likely only touch on a small portion of its capabilities, but as you dive deeper into scientific or technical fields, you'll find it a robust and convenient library.

NLTK

Natural Language Processing (NLP) is a subfield of artificial intelligence that focuses on the interaction between computers and humans through natural language. To work with human language, one needs the power of Natural Language Toolkit (NLTK), which is a leading platform for building Python programs to work with human language data.

NLTK is a powerful library that provides easy-to-use interfaces to over 50 corpora and lexical resources. It also includes a suite of text-processing libraries for classification, tokenization, stemming, tagging, parsing, semantic reasoning, and wrappers for industrial-strength NLP libraries.

One of the significant advantages of NLTK is the amount of resources, including documentation and plentiful example scripts, available to learn and understand it.

Using NLTK

Before you can use NLTK, you need to install it. You can do this with a simple pip command: pip install nltk. After installation, you can import NLTK into your Python environment.

```
# Importing NLTK

import nltk
```

To download specific NLTK packages or corpora, you can use nltk.download().

Here's an example of how to use NLTK for a basic NLP task - tokenization, which is the process of breaking down text into words, phrases, symbols, or other meaningful elements (known as tokens).

```
# Importing the tokenizer

from nltk.tokenize import word_tokenize


# Sample text

text = "NLTK is a leading platform for building Python
programs to work with human language data."


# Tokenize the text

tokens = word_tokenize(text)


print(tokens)
```

This script will output a list of individual words from the text:

```
['NLTK', 'is', 'a', 'leading', 'platform', 'for', 'building', 'Python',
'programs', 'to', 'work', 'with', 'human', 'language', 'data', '.']
```

The word_tokenize function from NLTK has split the sentence into individual words (tokens) and included punctuation as separate tokens.

Data Manipulation and Analysis

Numpy

NumPy (Numerical Python) is an open-source Python library that's used in almost every field of science and engineering. It's the universal standard for working with numerical data in Python, and it's at the core of the scientific Python ecosystem.

Understanding Arrays

NumPy's main object is the homogeneous multidimensional array. It's a table of elements (usually numbers), all of the same type, indexed by a tuple of positive integers.

```
import numpy as np

a = np.array([1, 2, 3])  # Creates a 1-dimensional array
```

Array Operations

NumPy, short for Numerical Python, provides powerful array operations that allow you to perform mathematical operations on arrays without the need for explicit looping. NumPy's array operations enable element-wise addition, subtraction, multiplication, and division between arrays, allowing you to perform calculations efficiently. For example, if you have two NumPy arrays A and B of the same shape, you can add them together simply by writing C = A + B, and NumPy will perform the addition operation on each corresponding pair of elements in the arrays. Similarly, you can perform subtraction (C = A - B), multiplication (C = A * B), and division (C = A / B) operations. Array operations in NumPy are highly optimised and can significantly improve the performance of numerical computations compared to traditional looping constructs.

Mathematical Functions

NumPy provides a wide range of mathematical functions that operate directly on NumPy arrays. These functions allow you to perform common mathematical operations, such as square roots, exponentiation, logarithms, trigonometric operations, and more, on entire arrays without needing to iterate over individual elements. For instance, if you have a NumPy array A, you can calculate the square root of each element by using the function np.sqrt(A). Similarly, you can calculate the exponential of each element with np.exp(A), calculate the natural logarithm with np.log(A), and perform various trigonometric functions like sine, cosine, and tangent using np.sin(A), np.cos(A), and np.tan(A), respectively. These mathematical functions provided by NumPy are optimised for numerical computations and can handle large arrays efficiently.

Statistical Functions:

NumPy also offers a variety of statistical functions that allow you to analyse data stored in NumPy arrays. These functions enable you to calculate common statistical measures such as the mean, median, standard deviation, variance, and more. For example, if you have a NumPy array A, you can calculate the mean using np.mean(A), the median using np.median(A), the standard deviation using np.std(A), and the variance using np.var(A). These statistical functions are handy when working with numerical data and analysing its properties. NumPy's statistical functions are designed to handle large arrays efficiently, making them suitable for processing large datasets and performing statistical analysis in scientific and data analysis applications.

Pandas

Pandas is a high-level data manipulation tool developed by Wes McKinney. It is built on top of the NumPy package and is widely used for data analysis and manipulation in Python. The key data structure provided by Pandas is called the DataFrame, which is a two-dimensional table-like structure that allows for efficient data manipulation.

Data Structures:

Pandas provides two main data structures: Series and DataFrame. A Series is a one-dimensional array-like object that can hold any data type, such as integers, floats, or strings. It is similar to a column in a spreadsheet or a single column in a database table. A DataFrame, on the other hand, is a two-dimensional tabular data structure that consists of multiple columns. It can be thought of as a combination of Series objects, where each column represents a Series. The DataFrame is the primary data structure in Pandas, and it allows for efficient handling and manipulation of structured data, similar to working with SQL databases.

Importing and Exporting Data:
Pandas provides functions to read and write data from various file formats and data sources. These functions enable you to import data from formats like CSV, Excel spreadsheets, SQL databases, JSON files, and more. Similarly, you can export data to different formats using Pandas, allowing you to save your processed data in a format suitable for further analysis or sharing with others.

Data Cleaning:
Pandas simplifies the process of cleaning and preparing your data for analysis. It provides a wide range of functions and methods to handle common data cleaning tasks, such as filling missing values, removing duplicates, dropping unused columns, handling outliers, and more. With Pandas, you can efficiently manipulate your data to ensure it is in a suitable format for analysis.

```python
import pandas as pd

# Let's assume the data looks like this:
data = {'Name': ['Tom', 'Nick', 'John', 'Tom'],
    'Score': [90, 85, None, 90]}
df = pd.DataFrame(data)

print("Original DataFrame")
print(df)

# Fill missing values with a specified placeholder
df['Score'].fillna(df['Score'].mean(), inplace=True)

# Remove duplicate rows
df.drop_duplicates(inplace=True)

print("\nCleaned DataFrame")
print(df)
```

Data Manipulation:

Pandas offers a powerful suite of data manipulation operations that allow you to transform and reshape your data. These operations include filtering and selecting data based on conditions, grouping data based on specific criteria, merging and joining multiple datasets, reshaping data between wide and long formats, and more. Pandas provides a flexible and intuitive syntax that simplifies complex data manipulation tasks, enabling you to efficiently explore and transform your data.

Data Visualisation:

While not a part of Pandas itself, Pandas integrates well with popular data visualisation libraries such as Matplotlib and Seaborn. These libraries allow you to create various types of visualisations, such as line plots, scatter plots, bar plots, histograms, and more, directly from your Pandas DataFrame. This integration enables you to easily visualise your data and gain insights through visual exploration, making it a powerful tool for data analysis and communication.

Both NumPy and Pandas are incredibly important libraries in Python for data analysis. Their abilities to handle and manipulate numerical data efficiently and flexibly make them indispensable tools for anyone dealing with data in Python.

Visualisation

Matplotlib

Matplotlib is a popular visualisation library in Python. It allows you to create static, animated, and interactive plots in Python.

Creating Plots:

You can create a variety of plots using Matplotlib, including line plots, bar plots, scatter plots, etc. Here's how to create a simple line plot:

```python
import matplotlib.pyplot as plt

x = [1, 2, 3, 4, 5]
y = [2, 4, 1, 3, 5]

plt.plot(x, y)
plt.show()
```

Customising Plots:

Matplotlib allows you to customise your plots extensively. You can add titles, labels for the x and y-axis, a legend, and more.

```python
import matplotlib.pyplot as plt
import numpy as np
# Generate some data
x = np.linspace(0, 10, 100)
y = np.sin(x)


# Create a figure and axis
fig, ax = plt.subplots()


# Plot the data
ax.plot(x, y, label='sin(x)', color='purple', linewidth=2)


# Customise the plot
ax.set_title('A Simple Plot')  # Add a title
ax.set_xlabel('X-Axis Label')  # Add an x-label
ax.set_ylabel('Y-Axis Label')  # Add a y-label


ax.legend()  # Add a legend


ax.grid(True)  # Add a grid


# Show the plot
plt.show()
```

Subplots:

Subplots allow you to place multiple plots in a single figure. You can do this using the subplots() function:

```
fig, axs = plt.subplots(2)

axs[0].plot(x, y)

axs[1].plot(y, x)

plt.show()
```

Seaborn

Seaborn is a Python data visualisation library based on Matplotlib. It provides a high-level interface for drawing attractive and informative statistical graphics.

Statistical Data Visualisation:

Seaborn comes with built-in datasets, functions to visualise regression models, and the ability to beautifully plot statistical time series. Some of its functions like distplot(), boxplot(), pairplot(), etc., make analysing data easier.

```
import seaborn as sns


tips = sns.load_dataset('tips')

sns.boxplot(x=tips['total_bill'])

plt.show()
```

Plotting Categorical Data:

Seaborn also makes it easy to visualise categorical data. Functions like catplot(), boxplot(), violinplot(), etc., are useful for this.

```
sns.catplot(x='day', y='total_bill', data=tips)

plt.show()
```

Both Matplotlib and Seaborn are powerful tools for creating insightful and compelling visualisations in Python. While Matplotlib provides a lot of flexibility, Seaborn simplifies common statistical plot types. Knowing how to use both of these libraries will allow you to present your data in clear and engaging ways.

Introduction to Web Scraping

Web scraping is a method used to extract a large amount of data from websites. It involves retrieving data from web pages and saving it to a local file on your computer or storing it in a database in a tabular format. Web scraping allows you to gather data from multiple web pages efficiently, automate data collection processes, and extract valuable insights from online sources.

Understanding HTML and CSS

HTML (Hypertext Markup Language) and CSS (Cascading Style Sheets) are two fundamental technologies used for building web pages. HTML provides the structure and content of a web page, while CSS defines the layout and visual styling of the page. To effectively scrape data from a website, it is important to understand how its HTML structure is organised and how CSS selectors are used to locate specific elements within the HTML code. This knowledge allows you to identify and extract the desired data from the web pages accurately.

For example, let's say we want to scrape the titles and prices of products listed on an e-commerce website. By examining the HTML structure of the website, we can identify the HTML tags and CSS classes that contain the relevant information. We might find that the titles of the products are enclosed in <h2> tags with a class of "product-title", and the prices are enclosed in <span> tags with a class of "product-price". With this information, we can write our web scraping code to target these specific HTML elements and extract the corresponding data.

Making HTTP Requests:

Before scraping a website, we need to send HTTP requests to retrieve the web pages' HTML content. In Python, the requests library is commonly used for making HTTP requests. With this library, we can specify the URL of the web page we want to scrape and send a GET request to retrieve the page's HTML content.

For example, using the requests library, we can send an HTTP GET request to a target website to retrieve its HTML content. The response from the website will include the HTML code of the requested page. We can then access and analyse this HTML code to extract the desired data.

Here's an example code:

```
import requests

url = 'https://www.example.com'
response = requests.get(url)


html_content = response.text


# Now we can process the html_content to extract the desired data
```

In this example, we specify the URL of the website we want to scrape and use the get() function from the requests library to send an HTTP GET request to that URL. The response object contains various properties and methods that allow us to access the response status, headers, and content. In this case, we access the HTML content of the response by calling the text property, which returns the raw HTML as a string.

Once we have obtained the HTML content, we can proceed to analyse and extract the desired data using techniques such as parsing the HTML structure, using CSS selectors, or leveraging additional libraries such as Beautiful Soup or Scrapy. These techniques allow us to navigate through the HTML code, locate specific elements, extract their content, and save it for further analysis or storage.

Web scraping provides a powerful way to collect and analyse data from websites, opening up opportunities for various applications such as market research, data analysis, sentiment analysis, and more. However, it's important to be mindful of website terms of service, legal restrictions, and ethical considerations while scraping data from websites.

BeautifulSoup

BeautifulSoup is a Python library specifically designed for web scraping tasks, allowing you to extract data from HTML and XML files in a straightforward manner.

Parsing HTML:
One of the key features of BeautifulSoup is its ability to parse HTML documents seamlessly. It automatically handles the conversion of incoming documents to Unicode and outgoing documents to UTF-8 encoding, relieving you from the burden of dealing with encoding complexities. BeautifulSoup can also detect the encoding specified in the document, ensuring accurate parsing. This means you can focus on extracting the data you need without worrying about encoding-related issues.

Navigating and Searching the Parse Tree:
Once you have parsed an HTML or XML document using BeautifulSoup, you can navigate and search the resulting parse tree to locate specific elements of interest. BeautifulSoup provides intuitive methods and Pythonic idioms to navigate and modify the parse tree. You can navigate the parse tree using the names of tags or attributes, allowing you to access specific elements directly. Additionally, BeautifulSoup offers powerful searching capabilities, enabling you to search for tags that match particular patterns. These navigation and search features make it easy to locate and interact with specific parts of the HTML or XML document.

For example, let's say you have parsed an HTML document using BeautifulSoup and want to extract all the links from the document. You can use the find_all() method to search for all the <a> tags in the document and retrieve their href attributes. This can be achieved with the following code snippet:

```
from bs4 import BeautifulSoup


# Assume 'html_content' contains the parsed HTML content

soup = BeautifulSoup(html_content, 'html.parser')
# Find all the <a> tags in the document

link_tags = soup.find_all('a')


# Extract the 'href' attributes from the <a> tags

links = [link['href'] for link in link_tags]


# Now you have a list of all the links in the HTML document
```

In this example, find_all('a') searches for all the <a> tags in the HTML document and returns a ResultSet object containing all the matching tags. By iterating over the ResultSet, we can extract the href attributes of the <a> tags, resulting in a list of links.

Extracting Data:

After locating the desired elements in the HTML or XML document, you may want to extract the data contained within those elements. BeautifulSoup provides various methods to retrieve the data, depending on the structure of the element and the desired outcome. For instance, you can use the get_text() method to retrieve all the text within an element, including the text from its child elements. This method concatenates the text of all the children into a single string.

Continuing from the previous example, if you want to extract the text from the <a> tags instead of the href attributes, you can modify the code as follows:

```
# Extract the text from the <a> tags

texts = [link.get_text() for link in link_tags]


# Now you have a list of all the text within the <a> tags in the
HTML document
```

By using the get_text() method on each <a> tag, we retrieve the text content within the tags and store it in the texts list.

BeautifulSoup simplifies the process of parsing HTML and XML documents and provides a clean and intuitive interface to navigate, search, and extract data from them. It is a valuable tool for web scraping tasks, enabling you to efficiently extract the desired information from web pages for further analysis or storage.

Selenium

Selenium is a powerful tool primarily used for automating browser tasks, often employed for testing purposes, but also utilised for web scraping tasks.

Automating Browser Tasks:

Selenium enables you to automate browser tasks by simulating user interactions. It provides a range of functionalities to interact with web pages programmatically, allowing you to perform actions like clicking buttons, filling out forms, scrolling, and navigating through web pages. Selenium essentially provides hooks and scripts that allow you to control and mimic the actions of a real user within a web browser.

Navigating Pages:

Selenium enables you to navigate to different web pages using the get() function. By specifying the URL of the desired web page, Selenium automatically loads that page in the browser. This functionality is useful when you need to scrape data from multiple pages within a website or follow specific links to access the desired content.

Filling Forms and Clicking Buttons:

Selenium can interact with form elements on a webpage, allowing you to fill out forms and submit data. You can locate form elements using HTML attributes such as IDs, classes, or names, and then send keystrokes to those elements programmatically. Similarly, Selenium provides the click() function to simulate clicking buttons or other clickable elements on a webpage.

Extracting Data:

Selenium's Webdriver API allows you to extract data from the HTML source code of a webpage. For example, if you want to extract the text inside a specific element, you can use the find_element_by_* methods to locate the element based on its attributes, and then access the desired data using attributes like text. This allows you to retrieve the text content, attributes, or other information from elements on the webpage.

```python
from selenium import webdriver

from selenium.webdriver.common.keys import Keys

from bs4 import BeautifulSoup

# Set up Selenium WebDriver

driver = webdriver.Chrome()    # Replace with the appropriate
WebDriver for your browser

# Open Google search page

search_query = "web scraping"

driver.get("https://www.google.com")

search_box = driver.find_element_by_name("search")

search_box.send_keys(search_query)

search_box.send_keys(Keys.RETURN)

# Wait for the page to load (you may need to adjust the wait time)

driver.implicitly_wait(5)

# Extract the page source and create a BeautifulSoup object

page_source = driver.page_source

soup = BeautifulSoup(page_source, "html.parser")

# Find the search results

search_results = soup.select("div.g")


#Continued….
```

```
# Process and print the titles and URLs of the search results

for result in search_results:

    title_element = result.select_one("h3")

    if title_element:

        title = title_element.get_text()

        link_element = result.select_one("a")

        if link_element:

            url = link_element["href"]

            print(f"Title: {title}")

            print(f"URL: {url}\n")

# Close the browser

driver.quit()
```

For instance, using Selenium, you can automate the process of logging into a website by locating the username and password fields, filling them in with the appropriate credentials, and clicking the login button. Additionally, you can scrape data from dynamic web pages that rely on JavaScript for rendering content. By automating the browser and letting it execute the JavaScript, Selenium ensures that you can access the fully rendered content and extract the desired data.

Selenium is a valuable tool for web scraping when the desired data cannot be easily accessed through traditional methods like parsing HTML. It provides the flexibility to interact with complex web pages, execute JavaScript, and extract data from dynamically generated content. Combining Selenium with other libraries like BeautifulSoup allows you to leverage the strengths of both tools for efficient and comprehensive web scraping tasks.

Intermediate Projects
A Simple Command-Line Application
Quiz Game

Let's dive into an engaging project that will utilise our Python knowledge - a Quiz Game.

- Project Idea: A Quiz Game: We'll create a simple quiz game that asks the user questions, takes input for answers, and provides a final score.

- Designing the Application: Our quiz game will include a list of questions with correct answers. The program will loop through these questions, ask them one by one, and compare user input with the correct answer.

- Implementing the Application: The basic code structure could look like this:

```python
def start_quiz(questions):
    score = 0
    for q in questions:
        answer = input(q.prompt)
        if answer == q.answer:
            score += 1
    print(f"You got {score}/{len(questions)} correct")

class Question:
    def __init__(self, prompt, answer):
        self.prompt = prompt
        self.answer = answer

questions = [
    Question('What is the capital of France?', 'Paris'),
    Question('Which is the largest ocean?', 'Pacific Ocean'),
    # Add more questions as needed
]

start_quiz(questions)
```

- Testing the Application: Make sure the game behaves as expected by playing it. Try different answers and edge cases (like what if the user enters something that isn't an option at all).

Web Scraping Project

Scraping a News Website

Now, let's turn our attention to a web scraping project - Scraping a News Website.

- Project Idea: Scraping a News Website: We'll create an application that can scrape news from a website and present the headlines to the user.

- Designing the Application: Our application will use BeautifulSoup to scrape data. We'll aim to extract headlines and maybe a short description or the news URL.
- Implementing the Application: Here's a very basic example of how you can implement this:

```
import requests

from bs4 import BeautifulSoup


def scrape_website(url):

    response = requests.get(url)

    soup = BeautifulSoup(response.text, 'html.parser')


    for headline in soup.find_all('h2'):    # the tag might be different depending on the website

        print(headline.get_text())


scrape_website('https://www.example.com')
```

- Testing the Application: Run the application with different URLs. Ensure that the application can handle possible exceptions and provides data in a clean, readable format.

In both projects, remember to handle exceptions and edge cases to make sure your application is robust and user-friendly. Code testing is a crucial part of the development process, so never overlook it. Always strive to improve and optimise your code where possible.

Data Analysis Project

Let's put into practice our knowledge of data analysis with Python, using libraries such as Pandas, Matplotlib, and Seaborn.

- Project Idea: Analysing a Dataset: We'll take a publicly available dataset (e.g., a dataset from the UCI Machine Learning Repository or Kaggle) and analyse it to extract meaningful insights. For example, we might use a dataset about the Titanic survival rates and analyse factors that influenced survival.
- Designing the Project: The first step is to understand the dataset and the kind of information it contains. We will identify which questions we want to answer. For the Titanic dataset, we might ask: What factors made people more likely to survive?
- Implementing the Project: We'll use Pandas for data manipulation and analysis. Here's a very basic example of how to start this analysis:

```python
import pandas as pd

# Load the data

data = pd.read_csv('titanic.csv')

# Explore the data

print(data.head())

print(data.describe())

# Clean the data (handle missing values, etc.)

# ...

# Analyse the data (this will depend on the questions you're trying to answer)

# For example, let's compare survival rates between men and women

print(data.groupby('Sex')['Survived'].mean())
```

- Visualising the Results: Data visualisation is a crucial part of data analysis. It allows us to better understand the data and to communicate our findings effectively. We can use libraries like Matplotlib and Seaborn to create our visualisations.

```
import matplotlib.pyplot as plt

import seaborn as sns


# Visualise survival rates between men and women

sns.barplot(x='Sex', y='Survived', data=data)
```

Always start by understanding your data and the questions you're trying to answer. Then, clean and preprocess your data before doing any analysis. Make your code modular and organised by dividing it into functions or classes each with a single purpose. Lastly, don't forget to visualise your results – good visualisations can make your conclusions much clearer and more impactful.

Introduction to Web Development with Python

Flask Framework

Flask is a lightweight web framework for Python that allows you to build web applications quickly and with ease. It is designed to be simple and minimalist, providing the basic tools and features necessary for web development while allowing developers the freedom to choose additional components and extensions as needed. Flask follows the principles of the Model-View-Controller (MVC) architecture, although it is often referred to as a microframework due to its simplicity and minimalistic approach.

Building a Simple Web Application

With Flask, you can quickly build a simple web application. The first step is to set up a Flask project by creating a new Python file. Within this file, you import the Flask module, create an instance of the Flask class, and define the routes and views for your application. Routes are URLs that users can visit, and views are Python functions that handle those requests and return responses. For example, you can define a route for the homepage ("/") and a corresponding view function that returns the content to be displayed on that page.

Routing and Templates:

Flask uses routing to map URLs to specific views or functions. You can define routes using decorators, which associate a URL with a particular view function. For instance, the @app.route('/') decorator can be used to define a route for the homepage. Additionally, Flask supports the use of templates to separate the presentation logic from the application logic. Templates allow you to dynamically generate HTML content by combining static HTML with placeholders and variables. Flask uses the Jinja templating engine, which provides powerful features such as template inheritance, loops, conditionals, and more.

Working with Forms and Databases:

Flask makes it easy to handle forms and interact with databases. You can define forms using Flask-WTF or other form libraries, allowing you to validate user input and process form data. Flask supports various database systems, and you can choose the one that suits your needs, such as SQLite, MySQL, PostgreSQL, or MongoDB. Flask integrates with popular database libraries, including SQLAlchemy and Flask-SQLAlchemy, providing an ORM (Object-Relational Mapping) layer that simplifies database interactions. With Flask and these libraries, you can perform database operations such as creating, reading, updating, and deleting records.

Here is a brief example of building a simple Flask application:

```python
from flask import Flask, render_template

app = Flask(__name__)

@app.route('/')
def home():
    return "Hello, Flask!"

@app.route('/about')
def about():
    return render_template('about.html')

if __name__ == '__main__':
    app.run()
```

In this example, we import the Flask module, create an instance of the Flask class named app, and define two routes using the @app.route() decorator. The home() function is associated with the root URL ("/") and returns a simple "Hello, Flask!" message. The about() function is associated with the "/about" URL and renders an HTML template using render_template().

The HTML template for the "about" page can be stored in a directory called "templates". For instance, the "about.html" template can include HTML code and placeholders for dynamic content.

Flask provides a development server, which can be started by calling app.run() when the script is executed directly. This server runs the Flask application and allows you to view it in a web browser.

Flask's flexibility, simplicity, and extensibility make it an excellent choice for developing web applications of various sizes and complexities. You can extend Flask's functionality by utilising various Flask extensions, such as Flask-WTF for form handling, Flask-SQLAlchemy for database interactions, Flask-RESTful for building REST APIs, and many more.

Django Framework

Django is a high-level web framework for Python that follows the Model-View-Controller (MVC) architectural pattern. It provides a complete set of tools and libraries for building web applications, making it highly efficient and suitable for projects of all sizes. Django follows the principle of "batteries included," which means it comes with many built-in features, including an ORM, authentication, URL routing, templating engine, and more. Django's primary goal is to help developers build complex web applications quickly and securely, with a strong emphasis on code reusability and maintainability.

Building a Simple Web Application

To get started with Django, you first need to set up a Django project. This involves creating a project directory and using the django-admin command-line tool to initialise a new Django project. Within the project, you define one or more Django apps that encapsulate specific functionalities or components of your web application. Django apps can be created using the manage.py script.

Models and the Admin Interface

Django provides a powerful Object-Relational Mapping (ORM) system, allowing you to define your application's data models as Python classes. These models represent database tables and include fields and relationships between them. Django's ORM abstracts the database operations, making it database-agnostic and providing a consistent API to interact with the database. The Django admin interface is automatically generated based on the defined models, providing an out-of-the-box interface for managing and manipulating the data stored in the database. This admin interface allows you to perform CRUD operations (Create, Read, Update, Delete) on the data with ease.

Views, Templates, and URLs

Django follows the Model-View-Template (MVT) pattern, which is similar to MVC. Views handle the business logic and interaction with models. Templates define the presentation layer and provide a way to generate dynamic HTML content. URLs map incoming requests to specific views, allowing users to access different pages of your web application. Django's URL routing system enables you to define URL patterns using regular expressions or named URL patterns. When a user visits a particular URL, Django uses the URL patterns to determine which view should handle the request and returns the corresponding HTML template as a response.

Here is a brief example of building a simple Django application:

Create a new Django project using the following command:

```
$ django-admin startproject myproject
```

Create a new Django app within the project:

```
$ python manage.py startapp myapp
```

Define the models in the models.py file within the app directory. For example:

```python
from django.db import models

class Book(models.Model):
    title = models.CharField(max_length=200)
    author = models.CharField(max_length=100)
    publication_date = models.DateField()

    def __str__(self):
        return self.title
```

Define the views in the views.py file within the app directory. For example:

```python
from django.shortcuts import render
from .models import Book

def book_list(request):
    books = Book.objects.all()
    return render(request, 'book_list.html', {'books': books})
```

Create the HTML template (book_list.html) within the app's templates directory. For example:

```html
<!DOCTYPE html>
<html>
<head>
  <title>Book List</title>
</head>
<body>
  <h1>Book List</h1>
  <ul>
  {% for book in books %}
    <li>{{ book.title }} - {{ book.author }}</li>
  {% endfor %}
  </ul>
</body>
</html>
```

Define the URL patterns in the urls.py file within the project directory. For example:

```
from django.urls import path

from myapp.views import book_list


urlpatterns = [

    path('books/', book_list, name='book_list'),

]
```

Run the development server:

```
$ python manage.py runserver
```

You can then visit http://localhost:8000/books/ in your browser to see the book list generated by Django.

Django provides extensive documentation and a rich ecosystem of packages and extensions, making it highly customisable and suitable for building complex web applications. It simplifies many common web development tasks and provides security features like built-in protection against common vulnerabilities. Django's emphasis on best practices and robustness makes it a popular choice for developing scalable and maintainable web applications.

Introduction to Machine Learning with Python

Scikit-Learn

Scikit-Learn, also known as sklearn, is a popular and powerful Python library for machine learning. It provides a wide range of algorithms, tools, and functionalities for various stages of the machine learning workflow, including data preprocessing, feature extraction, model selection, model evaluation, and more. Scikit-Learn is built on top of other scientific computing libraries such as NumPy and SciPy, making it a versatile and efficient choice for machine learning tasks.

Scikit-Learn follows a consistent and intuitive API design, which simplifies the process of developing machine learning models. Its well-documented and easy-to-use interface allows both beginners and experienced practitioners to leverage its capabilities effectively. Scikit-Learn's design philosophy emphasises code readability, ease of use, and code reusability, enabling developers to focus on the core machine learning concepts rather than getting lost in the implementation details.

Implementing a Simple Machine Learning Model:
To demonstrate how to implement a simple machine learning model using Scikit-Learn, we'll walk through an example of building a binary classification model. The goal is to predict whether an email is spam or not based on a set of features.

Step 1: Data Preparation

The first step is to prepare the data for training and evaluation. This includes importing the necessary libraries, loading the dataset, and splitting it into training and testing sets.

```python
import numpy as np
from sklearn.model_selection import train_test_split


# Load the dataset
X, y = load_data()


# Split the data into training and testing sets
X_train, X_test, y_train, y_test = train_test_split(X, y, test_size=0.2, random_state=42)
```

Step 2: Feature Engineering and Pre-processing

Next, we may need to pre-process and engineer the features to ensure they are in a suitable format for the machine learning model. This may involve scaling the features, handling missing values, or transforming categorical variables.

```
from sklearn.preprocessing import StandardScaler


# Scale the features

scaler = StandardScaler()

X_train_scaled = scaler.fit_transform(X_train)

X_test_scaled = scaler.transform(X_test)
```

Step 3: Model Selection and Training

Once the data is prepared, we can choose an appropriate machine learning algorithm and train the model using the training set.

```
from sklearn.metrics import accuracy_score


# Make predictions on the testing set

y_pred = model.predict(X_test_scaled)
```

Step 4: Model Evaluation

After training the model, we can evaluate its performance on the testing set to assess its accuracy and generalisation capabilities.

This example demonstrates the basic steps involved in implementing a machine learning model using Scikit-Learn. However, Scikit-Learn offers a wide range of algorithms and functionalities beyond logistic regression, allowing you to explore and experiment with different models and techniques to tackle various machine learning problems.

```
from sklearn.linear_model import LogisticRegression

# Create and train the model
model = LogisticRegression()
model.fit(X_train_scaled, y_train)
```

In summary, Scikit-Learn is a versatile and user-friendly library that simplifies the implementation of machine learning models in Python. Its extensive documentation, consistent API, and wide range of algorithms make it a valuable resource for both beginners and experienced practitioners. By leveraging Scikit-Learn's capabilities, you can focus on the core concepts of machine learning and develop robust models for a wide range of applications.

Machine Learning Basics

Understanding Supervised Learning

Supervised learning is a subfield of machine learning that deals with the training of models on labeled data. In supervised learning, we have a dataset that consists of input features (also called predictors or independent variables) and corresponding target variables (also known as labels or dependent variables). The goal is to learn a mapping function from the input features to the target variables, enabling the model to make predictions on unseen data.

The process of supervised learning involves two main steps: training and inference.

Training:

During the training phase, the model is presented with labelled examples. It learns from these examples by adjusting its internal parameters to minimise the difference between its predicted output and the true labels. This process is often referred to as optimisation or model fitting. The training data is divided into two subsets: the training set, used to train the model, and the validation set, used to tune the model's hyperparameters and assess its performance.

Supervised learning encompasses various algorithms, including:

- **Regression**: Used when the target variable is continuous or numerical. Regression models aim to find a mathematical relationship between the input features and the target variable. Examples include linear regression, polynomial regression, and support vector regression.

- **Classification**: Applicable when the target variable is categorical or discrete. Classification algorithms assign input data into predefined classes or categories based on their features. Common classification algorithms include logistic regression, decision trees, random forests, and support vector machines.

In supervised learning, the quality and representativeness of the training data are crucial factors that affect the model's performance. A well-prepared and balanced dataset can contribute to the model's ability to generalise well to unseen data.

Understanding Unsupervised Learning

Unsupervised learning is a branch of machine learning that deals with learning patterns and structures in data without explicit labels. Unlike supervised learning, there are no predefined target variables in unsupervised learning. Instead, the algorithms aim to uncover hidden patterns, relationships, and structures within the data.

Unsupervised learning algorithms primarily focus on two types of tasks: clustering and dimensionality reduction.

Clustering: Clustering algorithms group similar data points together based on their intrinsic characteristics or proximity in the feature space. The goal is to identify clusters or subgroups within the dataset. Common clustering algorithms include k-means clustering, hierarchical clustering, and DBSCAN (Density-Based Spatial Clustering of Applications with Noise).

Dimensionality Reduction: Dimensionality reduction techniques aim to reduce the number of input features while preserving important information and patterns in the data. This helps in visualising and analysing high-dimensional data, as well as reducing computational complexity. Popular dimensionality reduction algorithms include principal component analysis (PCA) and t-distributed stochastic neighbour embedding (t-SNE).

Unsupervised learning algorithms are often used for exploratory data analysis, pattern recognition, and data pre-processing tasks. They can help uncover hidden insights, identify anomalies or outliers, and provide a deeper understanding of the data's underlying structure.

Understanding Reinforcement Learning

Reinforcement learning (RL) is a branch of machine learning concerned with training agents to make sequential decisions in an environment to maximise a cumulative reward. In reinforcement learning, an agent learns by interacting with an environment and receiving feedback in the form of rewards or punishments. The agent's goal is to learn the optimal policy or strategy that maximises the long-term cumulative reward.

Key components of reinforcement learning include:

- Agent: The entity that interacts with the environment and learns from experience.
- Environment: The external context or system in which the agent operates.
- State: The representation of the environment at a particular time step.
- Action: The decision or choice made by the agent based on its current state.
- Reward: The feedback signal that indicates

Best Practices in Python

PEP8, also known as the Python Style Guide, is a set of guidelines and recommendations for writing clean, readable, and consistent Python code. It provides a standardised approach to coding style, naming conventions, and code organisation, making it easier for developers to collaborate and maintain Python projects.

PEP8 covers various aspects of coding style, including but not limited to indentation, line length, naming conventions, import statements, comments, and whitespace usage. Adhering to PEP8 helps improve code readability, which is essential for maintaining codebases and facilitating code reviews.

Formatting Your Code

To format your code according to PEP8 guidelines, you can follow these key principles:

1. **Indentation:** Use four spaces (not tabs) for each level of indentation. Consistent and clear indentation enhances code readability and ensures that the structure of your code is easily discernible.

2. **Line Length:** Limit lines to a maximum of 79 characters. This promotes readability, especially when code is viewed in different environments or on smaller screens. If necessary, you can break long lines into multiple lines using parentheses or backslashes.

3. **Naming Conventions:** Use descriptive names for variables, functions, classes, and modules. Variable names should be lowercase, with words separated by underscores (e.g., my_variable).

Function and method names should also be lowercase, with words separated by underscores (e.g., my_function). Class names should use CamelCase (e.g., MyClass). Module names should be lowercase with underscores (e.g., my_module.py).

4. **Import Statements:** Import statements should be placed at the top of the file, each on a separate line. Import only the necessary modules and avoid wildcard imports (from module import *). Organise imports in groups, with standard library imports first, followed by third-party library imports, and finally, local project imports.

5. **Comments:** Use comments to explain non-obvious sections of code, provide context, and document important details. Comments should be concise, clear, and written in complete sentences. Avoid excessive or redundant commenting.

6. **Whitespace Usage:** Use whitespace judiciously to enhance code readability. Add blank lines to separate logical sections of code. Leave a single space after commas, colons, and around operators to improve clarity. Avoid trailing whitespace at the end of lines.

Following these formatting guidelines helps maintain a consistent style across your Python codebase, making it easier to read, understand, and maintain. Several tools and editors provide automated code formatting tools (e.g., autopep8, black) that can help enforce PEP8 guidelines automatically.

Adhering to PEP8 is considered a best practice in the Python community, as it promotes code consistency and readability. By following these guidelines, you contribute to building maintainable, professional-grade Python code that is easily understandable and approachable by other developers.

Code Readability

Code readability refers to how easy it is for another programmer (or future you) to understand what your code is doing. This is crucial because software is often maintained and updated by people who didn't write the original code. If your code is hard to read, it makes their job difficult. Comments, descriptive variable names, and clear logical structure can all enhance readability.

Code Simplicity

Simplicity means that your code does exactly what it needs to do and no more. Unnecessary complexity can introduce bugs and make your code harder to understand and maintain. A common guideline here is KISS (Keep It Simple, Stupid!). This doesn't mean that you should avoid complex algorithms or design patterns when they're needed, but that you shouldn't add complexity without a good reason.

Code Reusability

Code reusability refers to the use of existing code to deliver functionality. Writing reusable code can save significant time and effort, reducing the chance of errors and making your code easier to maintain. Functions, classes, and modules can all aid in producing reusable code.

Writing Efficient Code

Understanding Time and Space Complexity

Understanding the time and space complexity of your code is essential for writing efficient algorithms. Time complexity measures how the runtime of an algorithm increases with the input size, while space complexity measures the amount of memory an algorithm requires.

By analysing the time and space complexity of your code, you can identify potential bottlenecks and optimise your algorithms accordingly. Common time complexity notations include Big O notation, such as O(1), O(n), O(n log n), O(n^2), etc. Space complexity is typically measured in terms of auxiliary space or memory usage.

Profiling Your Code

Profiling is the process of measuring and analysing the performance characteristics of your code to identify areas that can be optimised. It helps you pinpoint which parts of your code are consuming the most time or memory. Python provides various profiling tools that can assist in this process.

One commonly used profiling tool is cProfile, which is built into the Python standard library. It allows you to measure the execution time of each function and identify potential bottlenecks. Another popular option is line_profiler, which helps analyse line-by-line execution time to identify specific code segments that are causing performance issues.

Profiling your code helps you focus your optimisation efforts on the parts that have the most significant impact on performance.

Optimising Your Code

Once you have identified the performance bottlenecks through profiling, you can optimise your code using various techniques. Here are a few strategies to consider:

1. **Algorithmic Optimisation:** Consider optimising your algorithms to reduce time and space complexity. Look for more efficient algorithms or data structures that can solve the problem with fewer operations or lower memory requirements.

2. **Code Optimisation:** Review your code for any unnecessary operations or redundant calculations. Look for opportunities to simplify and optimise the logic. Use built-in functions or libraries instead of reinventing the wheel.

3. **Memory Optimisation:** Be mindful of memory usage. Avoid unnecessary data duplication and optimise data structures to minimise memory overhead. Consider using generators or iterators instead of materialising large datasets in memory.

4. **Caching and Memoization:** Use caching techniques to store and reuse computed results, particularly for expensive or repetitive computations. Memoization can significantly speed up computations by caching function results for specific input parameters.

5. **Vectorization:** Leverage vectorized operations and libraries like NumPy to perform computations efficiently on arrays or matrices. Vectorization avoids the need for explicit loops, leading to faster execution.

6. **Parallelisation:** Consider parallelising computationally intensive tasks by utilising multiple cores or processors. The multiprocessing

or concurrent.futures modules in Python provide convenient ways to achieve parallelism.

7. **Libraries and External Tools:** Utilise specialised libraries and external tools designed for performance-critical tasks. For example, Cython can be used to optimise Python code by compiling it to C or C++.

Remember, optimisation should be done judiciously. Focus on the critical sections of your code and measure the performance improvements with benchmarks or profiling tools. Maintain a balance between code readability and optimisation, as overly complex optimisations may hinder maintainability.

Debugging and Testing

Understanding Debugging

Debugging is the process of identifying and fixing errors or bugs in your code. It involves investigating and resolving issues that cause unexpected behaviour, incorrect results, or program crashes. Debugging is an essential skill for developers, as it helps ensure the correctness and reliability of software.

When encountering a bug, it is crucial to gather information about the problem. This can be done by examining error messages, using logging statements, or stepping through the code using a debugger. Understanding the context and reproducing the issue are important steps in the debugging process.

Debugging Techniques

Several techniques can aid in effective debugging:

1. **Print Statements:** Inserting print statements in your code can help track the values of variables and the execution flow. By strategically placing print statements at different stages, you can identify where the code deviates from the expected behaviour.

2. **Logging:** Utilise logging frameworks or libraries to capture important information during program execution. Logging allows you to record error messages, warnings, and informative messages at different severity levels. It provides a more structured approach compared to print statements.

3. **Debuggers:** Debuggers are powerful tools that allow you to step through your code, set breakpoints, and examine variables and their values at runtime. Integrated Development Environments (IDEs) often come with built-in debuggers, enabling you to trace the execution flow and identify problematic areas.

4. **Error Messages and Stack Traces:** When an exception occurs, error messages and stack traces provide valuable information about the cause and location of the error. Understanding how to interpret and use this information can help in identifying and fixing bugs.

Understanding Testing

Testing is the process of evaluating software to ensure it behaves as expected. It involves executing the code with different inputs and verifying the correctness of the output. Testing is crucial for verifying the functionality, performance, and reliability of software systems.

Testing can be categorised into different levels, including unit testing, integration testing, system testing, and acceptance testing. Each level has its own purpose and scope. In this chapter, we will focus on unit testing and integration testing.

Unit Testing

Unit testing involves testing individual units or components of code in isolation. A unit is the smallest testable part of the code, such as a function or a class method. Unit tests aim to verify the correctness of these units and ensure they behave as expected.

Unit testing frameworks like pytest or unittest provide tools for writing, executing, and automating tests. Test cases are written to cover different scenarios and edge cases, with the expected outcomes defined in assertions.

Unit testing helps catch bugs early in the development process and provides a safety net for refactoring or making changes to the codebase.

Integration Testing

Integration testing focuses on testing the interactions between different components or modules of the software system. It ensures that the integrated components work together as intended.

Integration tests can cover scenarios such as API endpoints, database interactions, or external service integrations. These tests validate the behaviour and communication between the components and detect issues that arise due to integration complexities.

Integration testing can be performed using testing frameworks, tools, or custom scripts that simulate the integration scenarios and verify the expected results.

By combining unit testing and integration testing, developers can establish a comprehensive testing strategy that validates the correctness and functionality of their code.

In conclusion, debugging and testing are integral parts of software development. Debugging helps identify and fix issues in the code, while testing ensures the reliability and correctness of the software. By employing effective debugging techniques and implementing a well-structured testing approach, developers can improve the quality of their code and deliver more robust and reliable software solutions.

Data Science

Python for Data Science

Python has become a popular programming language for data science due to its extensive ecosystem of libraries and tools. In this section, we will provide an overview of data science and highlight some essential Python libraries used in the field.

Overview of Data Science:

Data science involves extracting insights and knowledge from data through various processes, including data acquisition, cleaning, exploration, analysis, visualisation, and interpretation. It combines statistics, mathematics, and computer science to understand complex patterns, make predictions, and inform decision-making.

Python Libraries for Data Science:

1. **NumPy:** NumPy is a fundamental library for scientific computing in Python. It provides powerful array operations and mathematical functions, making it efficient for working with large, multi-dimensional arrays and matrices. NumPy forms the foundation for many other data science libraries.

2. **Pandas:** Pandas is a widely used library for data manipulation and analysis. It offers easy-to-use data structures, such as DataFrame and Series, which allow for efficient data cleaning, transformation, merging, and exploration. Pandas is invaluable for working with structured data.

3. **Matplotlib:** Matplotlib is a versatile library for data visualisation. It provides a wide range of plotting functions and customisation options to create various types of plots, including line plots, scatter plots, bar plots, histograms, and more. Matplotlib is highly customisable and integrates well with other libraries.

4. **Seaborn:** Seaborn is a high-level statistical plotting library that works well with Pandas data structures. It offers a simplified API for creating attractive and informative statistical visualisations. Seaborn is particularly useful for creating complex visualisations and exploring relationships in data.

5. **Scikit-Learn:** Scikit-Learn is a comprehensive library for machine learning in Python. It provides a wide range of algorithms for tasks such as classification, regression, clustering, and dimensionality reduction. Scikit-Learn also includes tools for model evaluation, cross-validation, and hyperparameter tuning.

6. **TensorFlow and Keras:** TensorFlow is an open-source machine learning framework developed by Google. It provides a flexible ecosystem for building and deploying machine learning models. Keras is a high-level neural networks API that runs on top of TensorFlow, simplifying the process of building and training deep learning models.

7. **Jupyter Notebooks:** Jupyter Notebooks are interactive, web-based environments for data analysis and prototyping. They allow you to write and execute Python code, view visualisations, and include text explanations. Jupyter Notebooks are widely used in data science for sharing and presenting data analysis workflows.

These are just a few examples of the many Python libraries available for data science. As you continue your journey in data science, you will likely encounter additional libraries and tools that suit your specific needs and interests.

Version Control Systems

Overview

Version Control Systems (VCS) are an indispensable part of modern software development, allowing teams to work on projects collaboratively without overwriting each other's changes. They track every modification to the code in a special kind of database, and if a mistake is made, developers can turn back the clock and compare earlier versions of the code to help fix the error.

The most widely used VCS in the programming world is Git. Git is an open-source, distributed version control system created by Linus Torvalds, the same person who created Linux. It was designed with the aim of handling everything from small to very large projects with speed and efficiency.

When you're using Git, you can think of your project directory as a workspace where you make changes to your files. Once you're satisfied with your changes, you stage them - this is like adding files to a box, ready to be shipped off. When you're ready, you make a commit, which takes the staged changes and stores them permanently in Git's database. In Git terms, this is like shipping off the box.

But where do you ship it to? This is where GitHub comes in. GitHub is a web-based hosting service for version control using Git. It's a platform where you can store your repositories online, enabling collaboration amongst your team members. It also provides a friendly interface for managing your Git repositories.

A repository, or "repo", is like a big file folder that contains all the files related to a project, as well as the history of all changes made to those files. When you create a repository on GitHub, it exists as a remote repository. You can clone this repository to create a local copy on your computer, and sync between the two locations.

Here are some basic Git commands:

- **git init:** Initialises a new Git repository and begins tracking an existing directory. It adds a hidden subfolder within the existing directory that houses the internal data structure required for version control.
- **git clone [url]:** Creates a local copy of a project that already exists remotely. The URL is the location of the remote repository.
- **git add [file]:** Stages a change. Git tracks changes to a developer's codebase, but it requires manual intervention to 'stage' any changes for commit (i.e., to add them to the 'box').

- **git commit -m "message":** Saves the staged content as a new commit in the history. This 'ships off the box.' The '-m' option allows you to add a message to your commit to describe the changes made.
- **git push:** Updates the remote repository with any commits made locally to a branch.
- **git pull:** Updates the local version of a repository from a remote.

- **git status:** Shows the status of changes as untracked, modified, or staged.
- **git log:** Displays the entire commit history using the default format. For customisation, 'git log --pretty=oneline' will show each commit on a single line.

Understanding Git and GitHub

The Git Workflow

At its core, Git is all about version control, allowing multiple developers to work on a project without conflict. To achieve this, Git employs a unique workflow with several stages. Here's a breakdown of a typical Git workflow:

1. **Working Directory:** This is your local project directory where you make changes to files.

2. **Staging Area (Index):** This is an intermediate area where changes can be reviewed and prepared before being committed to the repository.

3. **Local Repository:** This is the repository (database) on your local machine, storing all your commit histories.

4. **Remote Repository:** This is the repository stored on a remote server (like GitHub) that can be shared among multiple team members.

When you make changes in your working directory, Git recognises that changes have been made but won't record them until you tell it to. You do this by staging your changes with git add [file], which adds your modified files to the staging area. Once your changes are staged, you can commit them to your local repository using git commit -m "message". Your changes are now officially recorded in your project history!

The Power of GitHub

While Git is a command-line tool, GitHub provides a web-based graphical interface. It also provides access control and several collaboration features, such as wikis and basic task management tools for every project.

When your local repository is connected to a remote GitHub repository, your workflow expands:

5. **Push Changes:** After committing changes to your local repository, you can push these changes to your remote GitHub repository using git push.

6. **Pull Changes:** If others are also working on your project and have pushed their changes to the remote repository, you can pull their changes to your local repository with git pull. This is how teams can work on a project collaboratively without overwriting each other's work.

7. **Branching and Merging:** GitHub also simplifies the process of branching and merging. A branch is essentially a unique set of code changes with a unique name. The default branch name in GitHub is main. Once you've made changes on a branch and pushed them to GitHub, you can open a pull request to merge your changes into the main branch. Pull requests show content differences, or diffs, between the branches, and allow for further discussion before changes are merged.

8. **Forking:** This is a feature unique to GitHub. A fork is a copy of a repository that allows you to freely experiment with changes without affecting the original project. Once you've made your changes in your fork, you can issue a pull request to have them reviewed and possibly integrated into the original repository.

9. **Contributing to Open Source:** One of the biggest advantages of GitHub is how it facilitates open source contributions. If you find a project you're interested in, you can fork it, make changes, and propose those changes back to the original project.

Basic Algorithms and Complexity Analysis

Algorithms are the backbone of any software application. They provide a step-by-step procedure for calculations, data processing, and automated reasoning tasks. In this chapter, we will explore two fundamental types of algorithms—searching and sorting—and delve into the concept of complexity analysis using Big O notation.

Searching Algorithms

Searching algorithms are designed to retrieve information stored within some data structure. Here are two common searching algorithms:

- **Linear Search:** This is the simplest type of search algorithm. It works by examining each element in a list sequentially until the desired value is found or all elements have been checked. It's simple to implement but inefficient for large lists.

- **Binary Search:** This search algorithm works on the principle of divide and conquer and is much more efficient than a linear search. However, it requires the list to be sorted beforehand. Binary search works by repeatedly dividing the list in half and checking whether the desired value is in the first half or the second half of the list.

Sorting Algorithms

Sorting algorithms rearrange the elements in a list according to a specific order. Here are two commonly used sorting algorithms:

Bubble Sort: Bubble sort is a simple sorting algorithm that repeatedly steps through the list, compares adjacent elements, and swaps them if they are in the wrong order. This process repeats until no more swaps are needed.

Quick Sort: Quick sort is a divide and conquer algorithm. It works by choosing a 'pivot' element from the array and partitioning the other elements into two sub-arrays, according to whether they are less than or greater than the pivot. The sub-arrays are then recursively sorted.

Complexity Analysis (Big O Notation)

When choosing between algorithms, it's crucial to consider how they will perform as the size of the input grows. This consideration is called time complexity, often expressed using Big O notation.

Big O notation provides an upper bound of the complexity in the worst-case scenario, helping to quantify performance as the input size becomes large. Here are common time complexities:

- $O(1)$ denotes constant time complexity. No matter the size of the input data, the time taken remains constant.

- $O(n)$ denotes linear time complexity. As the input data size increases, the time taken to process the data increases linearly.

- $O(\log n)$ denotes logarithmic time complexity. The time taken increases logarithmically with the size of the input data. This is characteristic of algorithms like binary search.

- $O(n^2)$ denotes quadratic time complexity. The time taken is proportional to the square of the input data size. Bubble sort, for example, has a worst-case and average time complexity of $O(n^2)$.

Networking Basics

In today's interconnected world, understanding networking concepts is critical for any software developer. It's especially important to understand APIs (Application Programming Interfaces), which allow different software systems to communicate with each other. This chapter will introduce APIs, dive into RESTful API design, and explain how to work with APIs in Python using the Requests library.

Understanding APIs

APIs are sets of rules that dictate how software components should interact. APIs aren't specific to the web; they exist everywhere in the software world. However, when developers talk about APIs, they're usually referring to web APIs.

A web API allows different software systems to communicate over the internet. For example, when you use a mobile app, the app will use a web API to send your requests to a server. The server will respond with data, which the app can then display in a user-friendly way.

RESTful API Design

One common architecture style for designing networked applications is REST (Representative State Transfer). A RESTful API is an API that follows the principles of REST. Here are some key concepts:

- Resources: In REST, a resource is an object with a type, associated data, relationships to other resources, and a set of methods that operate on it. Resources are identified using URLs.

- HTTP Methods: REST APIs use standard HTTP methods, like GET, POST, PUT, DELETE, etc. For instance, a GET request is used to retrieve a resource, and a POST request is used to create a new resource.

- Stateless: Each request from a client must contain all the information needed by the server to understand and process the request. The server should not store anything between requests.

- Response Codes: REST APIs use standard HTTP status codes to indicate the success or failure of a request. For example, 200 means success, 404 means not found, and 500 means server error.

Working with APIs in Python (Requests Library)

Python has a built-in library called requests for making HTTP requests. Here is a basic example of how to use it:

```
import requests

# Send a GET request to a web API
response = requests.get('http://api.example.com/resource')

# Print the status code
print(response.status_code)

# Print the response data (as text)
print(response.text)
```

When we call requests.get, Python sends a GET request to the specified URL. The server's response is stored in the response object. We can then examine this object to see the server's response code and the data it sent back.

To install the requests library, you would typically use pip in the command prompt of your IDE:

```
pip install requests
```

Data Storage

In the world of programming, efficiently storing and retrieving data is crucial. This is where databases come into play. This chapter will introduce you to the basics of databases, touch on SQL, and show you how to interact with SQL databases using Python tools like SQLite and SQLAlchemy.

Understanding Databases

A database is a structured set of data. It helps in efficiently storing, handling, and retrieving data. Databases can be classified into two broad types - Relational databases and NoSQL databases.

Relational Databases are organised into tables, which are linked to each other based on relational models. Data is stored in rows in these tables. SQL (Structured Query Language) is predominantly used to manage and query data in a relational database.

NoSQL Databases are non-tabular and store data differently than relational tables. They're particularly useful for working with large sets of distributed data. NoSQL databases include MongoDB, Redis, and Cassandra, among others.

SQL Basics

SQL (Structured Query Language) is a standard language for managing and manipulating databases. SQL can be used to create, read, update, and delete (CRUD operations) database records. Here's a very brief overview:

- SELECT: Used to select data from a database. SELECT * FROM table_name; will select all data from table_name.

- INSERT INTO: Used to insert new data into a database. INSERT INTO table_name (column1, column2) VALUES (value1, value2);

- UPDATE: Used to update existing data within a table. UPDATE table_name SET column1 = value1 WHERE condition;

- DELETE: Used to delete existing data in a database. DELETE FROM table_name WHERE condition;

Working with SQL in Python (SQLite, SQLAlchemy)

Python provides several libraries to work with SQL databases. Two of the most commonly used ones are SQLite and SQLAlchemy.

SQLite is a C library that provides a lightweight disk-based database. It doesn't require a separate server process and allows accessing the database using a nonstandard variant of the SQL query language. It's included in the standard Python library. Here's a basic example of how to use it:

```
import sqlite3

# Connect to the SQLite database (or create it)
conn = sqlite3.connect('example.db')

# Create a cursor object
c = conn.cursor()

# Execute an SQL command
c.execute("CREATE TABLE stocks (date text, trans text,
symbol text, qty real, price real)")

# Commit the changes and close the connection
conn.commit()
conn.close()
```

SQLAlchemy is a SQL toolkit and Object-Relational Mapping (ORM) system that provides a full suite of well-known enterprise-level persistence patterns. It's designed for efficient and high-performing database access. Here's a basic example of how to use SQLAlchemy:

```
from sqlalchemy import create_engine


# Create an engine that stores data in the local directory

engine = create_engine('sqlite:///example.db')


# Execute the SQL command

engine.execute("CREATE TABLE stocks (date text, trans text,
symbol text, qty real, price real)")
```

Remember, this is a high-level overview of databases, SQL, and how Python interacts with SQL. The world of data storage is vast, with many nuances. However, understanding these basics is a solid first step in your journey as a database-savvy developer.

Introduction to Cloud Computing

Today, we have access to computing resources and services at our fingertips, all thanks to cloud computing. In this chapter, we will define what cloud computing is, introduce some services provided by prominent cloud providers, and touch upon how Python applications can be deployed to the cloud.

What is Cloud Computing?

Cloud computing is the delivery of various services through the internet. These resources include tools and applications like data storage, servers, databases, networking, and software. Instead of keeping files on a hard drive or local storage device, cloud-based storage makes it possible to save them to a remote database.

The key characteristics of cloud computing include on-demand self-service, broad network access, resource pooling, rapid elasticity, and measured service. This means you can access as much or as little as you need, and you only pay for what you use.

Services provided by Cloud Providers

There are several leading cloud providers, each offering a host of services. For our discussion, we'll focus on the "big three" - Amazon Web Services (AWS), Google Cloud Platform (GCP), and Microsoft Azure.

Amazon Web Services (AWS): AWS is a secure cloud services platform, offering compute power, database storage, content delivery, and other functionalities. Its well-known services include EC2 for virtual servers, S3 for storage, and RDS for relational databases.

Google Cloud Platform (GCP): Google Cloud is known for its machine learning and AI tools, as well as its speed and scalability. It also provides robust data storage and compute services, like Google Compute Engine and Google Cloud Storage.

Microsoft Azure: Azure is known for its excellent integration with other Microsoft products. It offers a wide range of solutions suitable for all kinds of applications. Key services include Azure Virtual Machines and Azure SQL Database.

While all these providers offer similar services, they each have their unique strengths and areas of specialisation. Your choice of provider will depend on your specific needs and circumstances.

Deploying Python Applications to the Cloud

Deploying Python applications to the cloud has become a routine task, thanks to the rich ecosystem of tools and services provided by cloud vendors.

Platform as a Service (PaaS): PaaS offerings like AWS Elastic Beanstalk, Google App Engine, or Azure App Service, manage the runtime, leaving developers free to focus on their applications. With just a few configuration tweaks, you can deploy your Python application directly to these platforms.

Containers and Orchestration: You can containerise your Python application using Docker, which makes it easy to create a consistent deployment unit that runs the same way everywhere. Once your application is containerised, you can use Kubernetes (available on all three major cloud providers) to orchestrate your container deployment.

Serverless: You can also go serverless, which means you don't have to manage any servers at all! You just write your Python function, and then deploy it to AWS Lambda, Google Cloud Functions, or Azure Functions. These services automatically scale to handle traffic patterns and only charge when the function is running.

In conclusion, cloud computing offers a transformative shift from running local servers to accessing high-end technologies on a pay-as-you-go basis. By understanding and harnessing these services, you can rapidly deploy your Python applications at scale, reaching a global audience in the process. This chapter provides just a glimpse into the vast world of cloud computing. As you delve deeper, you'll discover a wealth of tools and services that can help turn your Python code into powerful, scalable applications.

Concurrency and Multithreading

Concurrency and multithreading are critical concepts in modern programming. They allow you to execute multiple tasks at once, increasing the efficiency and performance of your programs. In this chapter, we'll introduce threads in Python, discuss Python's threading and multiprocessing modules, and touch upon AsyncIO.

Understanding Threads in Python

A thread is the smallest unit of execution in a program. Python, like many other languages, supports multithreading, where multiple threads can be spawned within a process, and each thread gets executed independently. However, due to Python's Global Interpreter Lock (GIL), only one thread can execute Python bytecodes at a time even on a multiprocessor system. Thus, threading is more suited for I/O-bound tasks (like downloading files from the internet) rather than CPU-bound tasks.

Using Python's threading and multiprocessing modules

Python provides two modules, threading and multiprocessing, that allow you to create and manage threads and processes.

The threading module lets you create threads, synchronise them, and control their execution. Here's an example:

```python
import threading
def print_numbers():
    for i in range(10):
        print(i)


def print_letters():
    for letter in 'abcdefghij':
        print(letter)


t1 = threading.Thread(target=print_numbers)
t2 = threading.Thread(target=print_letters)


t1.start()
t2.start()


t1.join()
t2.join()
```

In this example, t1 and t2 run concurrently. The start() method begins the execution of the threads, and join() ensures that the main program waits for both threads to finish before it continues.

However, due to the GIL, for CPU-bound tasks, multithreading may not provide the expected speedup. In this case, multiprocessing comes to the rescue.

The multiprocessing module bypasses the GIL by creating processes instead of threads. Each Python process gets its own Python interpreter and memory space so the GIL won't be a problem. Here's an example:

```python
import multiprocessing
def print_square(n):
    print("Square:", n * n)


def print_cube(n):
    print("Cube:", n * n * n)


p1 = multiprocessing.Process(target=print_square, args=(10,))
p2 = multiprocessing.Process(target=print_cube, args=(10,))


p1.start()
p2.start()
p1.join()
p2.join()
```

Python's asyncio is a library used for writing single-threaded concurrent code using coroutines, multiplexing I/O access over sockets and other resources, running network clients and servers, and other related primitives. It's different from threading and multiprocessing as it uses a single thread (the main thread) and uses non-blocking I/O calls.

Here's an example using asyncio:

```python
import asyncio

async def count():
    print("One")
    await asyncio.sleep(1)
    print("Two")

async def main():
    await asyncio.gather(count(), count(), count())

asyncio.run(main())
```

In this code, asyncio.gather runs three count coroutines concurrently. Each count coroutine waits for 1 second during its execution, but because of asyncio, they can run concurrently, and the total execution time is roughly 1 second.

In conclusion, understanding concurrency and multithreading is key for Python developers, especially when dealing with I/O-bound or CPU-bound tasks. These concepts help to create efficient and high-performing Python applications. As always, make sure to choose the right tool for your specific use case.

Introduction to GUI Programming

One of the significant benefits of programming is the ability to create visual applications with Graphical User Interfaces (GUIs). GUIs offer an interactive experience for users, making your programs easier to use. In this chapter, we'll introduce you to the world of GUI programming and guide you through the basics of creating GUIs with Python's built-in module, Tkinter.

What is GUI Programming?

GUI stands for Graphical User Interface. It's a type of user interface that allows users to interact with devices in a graphical way, with icons, buttons, sliders, and other visual indicators, as opposed to text-based interfaces, typed command labels, or text navigation.

GUI programming involves creating windows, buttons, text boxes, menus, scrollbars, and other elements, and then defining their behaviour. For example, you could define what happens when a user clicks a button, selects an item from a dropdown menu, or types text into a box.

Using Tkinter for Python GUIs

Python offers multiple options for GUI programming, but Tkinter is the one that's built into the Python standard library. It provides a powerful object-oriented interface to the Tk GUI toolkit, which is a cross-platform toolkit that ensures your applications look the same on Windows, Unix, and macOS.

Here's a simple example of a Python program with a Tkinter GUI:

```python
from tkinter import Tk, Label

# Create a new Tk root window
root = Tk()

# Create a label widget
label = Label(root, text="Hello, Tkinter!")

# Add the label to the root window
label.pack()

# Start the event loop
root.mainloop()
```

In this code, we first import the necessary modules. Then we create a root window. The Label widget is created and added to the root window with the pack() method. The call to mainloop() starts the event loop, which waits for events such as button clicks or key presses.

Although this example is straightforward, Tkinter can be used to build complex, multi-window applications with menus, text fields, buttons, checkboxes, canvases for drawing, and other widgets.

GUI programming may seem daunting if you're used to text-based programming, but it opens a whole new world of possibilities for user interaction. Remember, like any other skill, proficiency comes with practice. Start small, be patient, and have fun building your own graphical interfaces.

Secure Coding Practices

Understanding Security in Programming

As our world becomes increasingly digitised, understanding security in programming is no longer a luxury – it's a necessity. Poorly written software can be an easy target for malicious hackers who are looking for ways to exploit vulnerabilities, steal data, and wreak havoc. With Python being one of the most popular programming languages, securing your Python code is critical. This chapter aims to provide a foundation for security principles in Python programming.

Security Principles

The basics of secure programming include principles like least privilege, defense in depth, and input validation.

Least Privilege: This principle states that a process should only have the minimum privileges needed to perform its tasks. By following this principle, even if an attacker gains control of a process, they will only have limited access to the system.

Defense in Depth: This principle advocates having multiple layers of security so that if one fails, others still stand. For example, even if your application code is secure, you should still have network-level security controls.

Input Validation: This is an essential aspect of secure programming. Always validate and sanitise user inputs to protect against threats like SQL injection and cross-site scripting (XSS).

Securing Your Python Code

Python, like other languages, has potential security pitfalls. Here are some recommendations for writing secure Python code.

Avoid using eval() and exec(): These functions evaluate Python expressions from strings, which can pose a significant security risk if the string comes from an untrusted source. If possible, use safer alternatives such as ast.literal_eval().

Beware of insecure modules and functions: Some Python modules and functions can pose a security risk if used incorrectly. For example, the pickle module can execute arbitrary code during deserialisation, making it a dangerous choice for handling untrusted data.

Update Python and its libraries regularly: Python, like other software, is updated regularly to fix security vulnerabilities. Always ensure you're using the latest version of Python and its libraries.

Use a Static Code Analyser: Tools like Bandit or PyLint can help identify common security issues in your Python code.

Handling Sensitive Data

As a Python developer, you might need to handle sensitive data such as passwords, API keys, or cryptographic keys. It's essential to manage this data securely. Avoid hard-coding sensitive data in your code, use Python's secrets module for generating secure random numbers for managing secrets, and consider encryption for storing sensitive data.

Web Security

If you're developing a web application with Python, understanding web security is vital. You need to be aware of threats like SQL Injection, XSS, and Cross-Site Request Forgery (CSRF), and know how to mitigate them. Frameworks like Django and Flask have built-in protections against many common attacks, but it's still crucial to understand these threats to use those protections effectively.

Secure Network Communications

For network communications, use secure protocols like HTTPS or secure versions of FTP and SSH. Libraries like requests make it easy to interact with HTTPS websites.

To conclude, while Python is a relatively safe language, no language can protect against poor security practices. A solid understanding of security principles and the common pitfalls in Python programming will go a long way in protecting your code from potential threats. Be aware that security is an ever-evolving field – always continue to learn and keep up-to-date with recent developments and vulnerabilities. Remember, the goal is to develop not just functional, but secure Python applications.

Common Security Vulnerabilities

SQL Injection

SQL Injection (SQLi) is an attack technique where an attacker inserts malicious SQL code into a query. It typically occurs when your code uses input to create SQL queries without proper sanitisation. If successful, an SQLi attack can have severe consequences, including unauthorised data access, data corruption, or even data loss.

For example, consider a login form where the underlying code uses user input to construct a SQL query:

```
query = f"SELECT * FROM users WHERE username='{username}' AND password='{password}'"
```

An attacker could input a value like ' OR '1'='1 for both username and password, altering the query to return all users, effectively bypassing the login mechanism.

To prevent SQLi, always use parameterised queries or prepared statements. Most Python database libraries support this. For instance, in SQLite:

```
c.execute("SELECT * FROM users WHERE username=? AND password=?", (username, password))
```

Cross-Site Scripting (XSS)

XSS is an attack that injects malicious scripts into webpages viewed by other users. It typically occurs when your application includes untrusted data in a new web page without proper HTML escaping.

For example, if your site has a comment section that directly inserts user comments into the page HTML, an attacker could post a comment containing a script tag with malicious JavaScript. Every user who views the comment would then execute the script.

To mitigate XSS attacks, always escape user input and never insert untrusted data directly into your HTML. Modern web frameworks, including Django and Flask, have built-in protections against XSS.

Cross-Site Request Forgery (CSRF)

CSRF is an attack that tricks the victim into submitting a malicious request. It exploits the trust a site has in a user's browser. For instance, if a user is logged into a web application, another site can force the user's browser to make a request to the web application on their behalf without their consent.

For example, an attacker could create a malicious site that automatically submits a form to your site to change the user's email address. The browser would include any cookies associated with your site, which would include the user's session cookie if they are logged in, making the request appear legitimate.

To mitigate CSRF attacks, use anti-CSRF tokens. These are random values associated with the user's session, included in every state-changing form or AJAX request. Before processing any state-changing request, the server checks that the request includes the expected token. Django and Flask both have built-in protections against CSRF.

Deployment
Bringing Your Python Application to Life

Writing your Python code is just the first half of the journey in software development. Once your code is written, tested, and debugged, it's time to deploy it. Deployment is the process of making your application available for use in a live environment, which could be a production or staging environment.

What is Deployment?

In a broader sense, deployment involves all the activities that make a software system available for use. In the case of Python, this could mean deploying a web application to a server, publishing a package for others to use, or even delivering a script to run on a specific machine.

There are many ways to deploy a Python application, from running a script on a local machine, using a dedicated web server, to leveraging cloud-based platforms.

Deployment Tools: Docker

Among the various tools and platforms available for deployment, Docker is one of the most popular. Docker is an open-source platform that automates the deployment, scaling, and management of applications. It uses containerisation technology to package an application along with its runtime environment, so it can run uniformly across different systems.

Understanding Docker

The core concept behind Docker is the use of containers. A container packages an application's code, configurations, and dependencies into separate building blocks. This means that the application can run reliably and consistently across different computing environments.

Unlike virtual machines, Docker containers do not have a full operating system; instead, they share the OS kernel of the host machine, which makes them lightweight and efficient.

Using Docker for Python Applications

To use Docker, you must first install Docker Desktop on your machine. Once installed, you can containerise your Python application by creating a Dockerfile. This file instructs Docker on how to build an image of your application.

Here is a basic Dockerfile for a Python application:

```
# Use an official Python runtime as a parent image
FROM python:3.7-slim


# Set the working directory in the container to /app
WORKDIR /app


# Add the current directory contents into the container at /app
ADD . /app


# Install any needed packages specified in requirements.txt
RUN pip install --no-cache-dir -r requirements.txt


# Make port 80 available to the world outside this container
EXPOSE 80


# Run app.py when the container launches
CMD ["python", "app.py"]
```

You can build the Docker image by running the docker build command in your terminal and then run your application with docker run.

Ethics in Programming

Ethics in programming might not be the first thing that comes to mind when you think about coding. However, as the influence of technology continues to grow, so does the need for ethical considerations in the creation and deployment of software.

The Need for Ethics in Programming

As a programmer, you have the power to create systems and tools that can have a broad impact on individuals and societies. With this power comes a responsibility to consider the ethical implications of what you create. Your code may be used in ways you never imagined, and even small oversights can result in serious consequences. Thus, it's important to consider ethics as an integral part of the programming process.

Respecting Privacy

In an era where data is gold, respecting user privacy is a significant ethical concern. Personal data can reveal a lot about an individual, and misuse can lead to serious invasions of privacy. As programmers, we must take care to only collect the data we need, to secure it properly, and to respect user's decisions about how it's used.

For instance, if you're building an application that requires user information, ensure that the data collection is transparent and consent is explicitly given. Always use secure methods to store and transmit user data, and respect the laws and regulations around data privacy in the regions where your application is used.

Avoiding Harm

Another primary ethical concern is the potential for harm. This can come in many forms, ranging from security breaches to job displacement due to automation. As programmers, we must strive to foresee and mitigate the potential negative impacts of the software we build.

For instance, it's important to thoroughly test and debug software before release to minimise the risk of bugs causing harm. On a larger scale, when building systems that may replace human labour, it's essential to consider the potential societal impacts.

Algorithmic Bias and Fairness

With the growing use of algorithms and AI in decision-making, another ethical concern is algorithmic bias. Algorithms trained on biased data can perpetuate and amplify existing inequalities. As programmers, we must understand the potential for bias in the data we use, and strive to develop algorithms that are fair and transparent.

Open Source and Collaboration

Many programmers contribute to open-source projects as a way to give back to the community. However, this comes with its own ethical considerations. We must respect the licenses of other people's code and give credit where credit is due.

Creating a web application

As mentioned before, you can download Python from https://www.python.org/downloads/, and Flask can be installed via pip, a package manager for Python:

```
pip install flask
```

Step 1: Set up your project

1.1. First, create a new folder on your computer where you'll store your project. You can do this via the terminal or manually. Let's call it "bookstore".

1.2. Open Visual Studio Code (VS Code). You can download it from https://code.visualstudio.com/download if you haven't installed it yet.

1.3. Once VS Code is open, go to File -> Open Folder and select the "bookstore" folder you just created.

Step 2: Creating the Flask application

2.1. Create a new file in the "bookstore" folder. To do this in VS Code, right-click on the folder name in the left panel and select "New File". Name this file "app.py".

2.2. In "app.py", we'll start by importing Flask and creating a new Flask web server from the Flask module:

```
from flask import Flask

app = Flask(__name__)
```

2.3. We'll define a route for our web application. Routes determine the URLs that our application responds to. Add the following code below the previous lines:

```
@app.route('/')

def home():

    return "Welcome to our Online Bookstore!"
```

This code creates a new route for the URL "/", the homepage for most websites. When someone visits this URL, the message "Welcome to our Online Bookstore!" will be displayed.

Step 3: Running the application

3.1. To run the application, we need to add the following lines at the end of "app.py":

```
if __name__ == '__main__':

    app.run(debug=True)
```

This line states that if we're running this file directly (i.e., not importing it from another script), we should run the Flask web server.

3.2. You can now run the app from the terminal integrated in VS Code. To open it, go to Terminal -> New Terminal. Make sure the terminal's path is in the "bookstore" folder.

3.3. In the terminal, type python app.py to start your Flask app. You should see output telling you that the server is running, along with the address it's running at (typically http://127.0.0.1:5000/). Open this address in your web browser, and you should see your application running.

Step 4: Expanding the Application

For a real bookstore, we need more than just a homepage. We might have a page that lists all the books, individual book pages, etc. We can create these as new routes in our Flask application.

4.1. Let's add a route that lists books. Add a new route above our if statement:

```
@app.route('/books')

def books():

    return "Here is a list of books."
```

4.2. If you visit http://127.0.0.1:5000/books in your web browser now, you will see the text "Here is a list of books."

This application is just a basic starting point. From here, you could extend the app by adding a database to store your book data using SQLAlchemy, improve the UI with templates using Jinja2, and much more.

The Journey of Learning Python and Beyond

As we wrap up this comprehensive introduction to programming in Python, it is vital to remember that the journey of learning does not stop here. Programming, much like any other field, is a lifelong pursuit of knowledge and improvement. You've equipped yourself with a solid foundation, but the world of Python, and programming in general, is vast and continually evolving.

The beauty of programming lies not only in the tangible applications you can create but also in the way it shifts your mindset. It encourages problem-solving, analytical thinking, and creativity, skills that are valuable across many aspects of life.

Remember that Python is just one language in a world filled with diverse programming languages. Now that you have a grasp of Python and its applications, you can explore other languages with relative ease. Each language has its strengths and ideal use-cases, and a versatile programmer can leverage these to choose the best tool for the job.

In this book, we've covered a wide array of topics, from understanding the basics of Python to exploring its application in web development, data analysis, machine learning, and more. We have dived into algorithms, databases, and cloud services. However, the technologies we discussed are part of a broader ecosystem. Keep exploring and keep learning.

As you continue your journey, keep in mind the importance of good coding practices. Write clean, efficient, and secure code. Use comments to document your work and make it understandable for others (including a future version of yourself). Test your applications thoroughly and strive for continuous improvement. And don't forget the role of ethics in programming - respect privacy, avoid harm, ensure fairness, and contribute positively to the programming community.

One of the most effective ways to learn and improve is by doing. Work on projects that excite you. There's no better way to consolidate your knowledge than by applying it to real-world scenarios. Share your work and collaborate with others. Engage with the vibrant Python community, contribute to open-source projects, and learn from the work of others.

Remember that it's okay to not know everything and to make mistakes. It's all part of the learning process. Take on challenges, solve problems, and when you get stuck, don't hesitate to ask for help. There are numerous resources available to assist you, from documentation and forums to videos and tutorials.

In conclusion, be proud of how far you've come. Learning to program is a significant achievement, and you're now part of an exciting world filled with possibilities. This book has given you the tools, knowledge, and confidence to get started, but the rest is up to you. Keep coding, keep learning, and most importantly, have fun along the way.

Here's to your success in your coding journey.

www.ingramcontent.com/pod-product-compliance
Lightning Source LLC
LaVergne TN
LVHW051653050326
832903LV00032B/3779